PRAISE FOR *I'm Not Crazy, I'm Just Not You*

"*I'm Not Crazy, I'm Just Not You* is a tool for the umes. This book helps individuals and managers understand how to communicate through the differences among us, for swifter consensus, more dependable decision making, with higher trust and understanding among the workgroup."

Jim Herbert
Cofounder, Association Management Bureau
Executive Director, International Teleconferencing Association

"This innovative, yet immensely practical, book provides a refreshing depth of insight into the complexities of normal human behavior. Quite simply, this is one of the best books on psychological type that I've read in the last twenty years. Must reading for everyone committed to helping others realize their full, human potential."

Charles C. Schroeder
Vice Chancellor for Student Affairs, University of Missouri-Columbia
Past President, American College Personnel Association

"Pearman and Albritton have created fresh insights into the 'fundamental threads of humanity' that weave through all of our lives. The reader will encounter a thought-provoking means of contemplating the courageous life and options for personal growth, and gain an understanding of the life tasks that are common to all mature human beings."

Gordon Patterson
Trainer
Center for Creative Leadership

"This book should serve as a wake-up call for all to reevaluate how they behave and interact. I found *I'm Not Crazy, I'm Just Not You* personally and professionally enlightening and would recommend it to everyone with the desire to grow and improve."

Amanda Canavan
Senior Project Administrator
Wachovia Bank & Trust

I'M NOT CRAZY

I'M JUST NOT YOU

I'M NOT CRAZY
I'M JUST NOT YOU

The Real Meaning of the 16 Personality Types

ROGER R. PEARMAN

■

SARAH C. ALBRITTON

DAVIES-BLACK PUBLISHING

Palo Alto, California

Published by Davies-Black Publishing, an imprint of
Consulting Psychologists Press, Inc., 3803 East Bayshore
Road, Palo Alto, California 94303; 1-800-624-1765.

Special discounts on bulk quantities of Davies-Black
Publishing books are available to corporations, profes-
sional associations, and other organizations. For details,
contact the Director of Book Sales at Davies-Black
Publishing, 3803 East Bayshore Road, Palo Alto,
California 94303; 415-691-9123; Fax 415-988-0673.

01 00 99 98 97   10 9 8 7 6 5 4 3 2 1
Printed in the United States of America

Library of Congress Cataloging-in-Publication Data
Pearman, Roger R.
        I'm not crazy, I'm just not you : the real meaning of
    the 16 personality types / by Roger R. Pearman and
    Sarah C. Albritton.
            p. cm.
        Includes bibliographical references and index.
        ISBN 0-89106-096-0
    1. Typology (Psychology)   2. Myers-Briggs Type
    Indicator.   I. Albritton, Sarah C.   II. Title.
    BF698.3.P43   1997
    155.2′64—dc20
                                                    96-43662
                                                        CIP

FIRST EDITION
First printing 1997

To our children
Olivia, Luke, Wells, Eliza, and Emmy

May your discoveries lead you to joy

CONTENTS

*W*hat is "normal" human behavior? When we are troubled or amazed by what others do, we often remark, either with a furrowed brow or a gasp of delight, "It's just not normal to be able (or willing) to do that." We sometimes even hear the remark, "It's not normal to be so normal!" Some people just can't win the normalcy game. Even when we know intellectually that there are many ways to be normal, we still compare ourselves to friends, neighbors, colleagues, and celebrities, using them as a kind of personal checkpoint as if to say, "Compared to that person, I'm pretty normal." But just when we allow ourselves to feel comfortable, we may find ourselves in disagreements, experiencing disappointment, or mired in confusion because we misunderstood, or were misunderstood by, someone else. Our version of normality meets resistance from other normal people. Such moments cause many of us to pause and try to figure out what happened to make things go wrong. We may find ourselves muttering, "It seemed like a reasonable request to me; why did she look at me as if I were crazy?" or "I was just trying to be helpful and considerate! Why do I suddenly feel like I made a terrible mistake?" or "I worked hard to prepare a thorough presentation. Why did they keep asking questions that were irrelevant and outside the scope of what I was asked to do?" In essence, the situational question we perpetually ask is: What behavior in this setting will seem normal, reasonable, and acceptable? It troubles us how and why such differences of perspective occur and, if truth be known, we really want to know if one perspective is more right than the other.

Compounding, and too often confounding, the search for normalcy are the many so-called self-help and pop psychology books. These are often based solely on one person's experiences, but writ large enough to make those experiences seem normal and therefore applicable to you and me. Even self-help books that are not anecdotal are often based on research that, even if sound, has been conducted on a "clinical population." In other words, the people who were studied and on whom a book's assumptions are based are people who participated in a study because they were seeking professional help for an emotional or psychological problem.

Then, the well-meaning psychologist or psychiatrist writes a book about what treatment helped these people, often neglecting to mention that if the reader isn't troubled by the same problem to the point of seeking professional help, the remedy in the book isn't likely to be a good fit. Further, these authors often make assumptions about "the rest of us " based on a small sample of people with admitted problems. Given the popularity of some of these books, it seems that true normality just doesn't sell to the reading public.

So, where is a description of regular folks with regular jobs trying the best they can to make the most of themselves, their families, and their lives? Where are some responses to life's everyday questions such as: Why do my spouse or kids and I consistently argue about this kind of thing? Why can't I get my ideas across to my boss, or to the other members of the volunteer group I work with? How can I learn to be a better listener and a better communicator in general? Why is this project so energizing while others are so draining?

We hope that in this book you will find some answers, or at least a clear road map to lead you to them. It is our attempt to identify and discuss the many layers and levels of ideas about normal human behavior found in the dynamic personality theory called *psychological type.*

This theory of human behavior is based on sixty years of observation and research. Our work with psychological type began in 1978 and continues today. In our careers as career counselors, therapists, managers, trainers, and later as corporate development specialists, we have used psychological type when appropriate to help individuals make career decisions, work through personal development issues, and become more effective managers and team members. Over nearly two decades we have trained or worked with thousands of individuals who, through an understanding of psychological type, have come to understand themselves and honor their own brand of "normal." We will inform you of knowledge that we believe is substantiated by sound research (not anecdotal or based on purely personal experience) and helpful to the average person. A bit of history and background provides the context for this effort.

In 1921, Swiss psychologist/anthropologist/man of letters Carl Gustav Jung wrote *Psychological Types,* a book based on his extensive study of many varied cultures, both ancient and modern. The majority of the book is an anthropological treatment of how these cultures defined and described normal human behaviors. He described all the major trends and insights about personality, and offered his own modern-day explanation for two basic questions. First, how do normal human beings take in information—how do they know things? He called this dimension of personality *perception*. Second, how do normal human beings make decisions or judgments about things? He called this dimension *judgment*. Overlying these two core questions about mental functioning was a third dimension dealing with the question of where people get and expend their energy.

At about the same time, an American mother/daughter team was asking the same kinds of questions. Katharine Briggs and Isabel Briggs Myers were studying and writing about why different sorts of people succeed or fail at different jobs. When they read Jung's work, they found that it embodied all their ideas and more. They then began what became the lifelong task of bringing every-day application and understanding of Jung's insights to the general public—to normal people. They felt that if an instrument could be designed to help people identify their preferred perceiving and judging styles and the source of their energy, the insights gained would help us to value ourselves and others more highly. They hoped that, with this knowledge, people could have more satisfying and successful educational and vocational experiences, as well as improved relationships. With these ideals to guide them, they spent the next twenty years developing what is now known as the *Myers-Briggs Type Indicator®* personality inventory, more commonly referred to as the MBTI®.

So innovative were their insights that their work has unleashed three decades of study and application in religion, man-agement, education, counseling, and human relations. Since its first publication in 1962, the MBTI is now the most widely used psychological instrument in the world. It has been translated into more than thirty languages, and to date an average of five million people per year take the MBTI in some setting or another. To our knowledge, Jung's model of psychological type, as embodied in the MBTI, is the only theory of human psychology that is based on nor-mal populations and that emphasizes the constructive use of dif-ferences, rather than simply classifying and defining differences as matters of good-better-best or normal-abnormal outcomes.

Jung's notion, honored in Myers and Briggs' work, is that the different styles of perception, judgment, and energy flow are just that—different. One is not inherently better or worse than another. Society may not take kindly to a model in which everybody wins, but it is our contention that this model is the key to successfully navigating the future. This deeply held belief is our motivation for writing. For if as individuals, families, communities, and societies we cannot learn to see value in the differing views and resources of others, we are surely lost.

You might well ask at this point why you need to read this book. First, all around us we can see that human beings are struggling with the issue of valuing differences. This book, at its core, is about how we can identify, understand, and value human differences in constructive and productive ways. The better you understand your own natural tendencies and how they get expressed in your behavior, the easier it is to understand those things that you take for granted and/or assume are as true for others as they are for you—your interpersonal blind spots. This understanding enables you to attend to your own personal development needs, thus freeing you from the nagging fear, "What have I missed in this interaction?" With an understanding of type, you'll have a very educated guess about what is in your blind spot and can then take proactive steps to compensate. Just as important as what you learn about yourself is what you can learn about others. You may become aware of the dynamics and patterns natural to each individual; thus, you can learn to truly appreciate the richness of differences.

Second, we firmly believe you will find in these pages information that will aid you in every aspect of life—working, loving, parenting, and dealing with others. We have included many personal stories from our families, our work, and our volunteer experiences that we feel illustrate the important points. Yes, these are anecdotal, but take them in the spirit in which they are offered—not as glaring, bells-and-whistles events that only happen to special people, but as gentle teaching tales. You too can begin to notice similar incidents in your life if you start to keep your "type lenses" on. We will repeat over and over that type does not explain everything in human behavior and interaction. Far from it. But there is a pervasive quality about type that we and many others find intriguing, helpful, and often transformative. We hope our work can help you see that, too.

A final piece of groundwork before we dive into these important matters. As we have obviously taken issue with the generalities made from the research base in some other books, you should rightly be wondering about the nature of the research upon which we have based this work. Research into normal human behavior is a compelling enterprise. Researchers must make sure that those participating in the research represent regular, everyday people. As discussed earlier, for answers to questions about normal human behavior it is not helpful to study patients in mental health institutions or long-term therapy and then generalize the results to the rest of us. So, assuming the sample is a representative group of people, researchers next have to be sure that the way data are gathered and analyzed makes sense. Have other influences on behavior been reasonably accounted for? Was the research setting nonthreatening and nonbiased? We made sure that these and many other more technical questions were answered appropriately before we included the results of any piece of research in our work.

Research Base

The research that we have drawn on here comes from studies conducted all over the globe. We looked at research on everyday issues like stress, management behaviors and psychological type. Each research piece used the MBTI and some other measure of behavior. When we found that at least three different studies suggested the same qualities about a type, we used the descriptors to present to participants in our workshops. After presenting programs all over the United States and Canada, we found that the descriptors were confirmed by folks of those types from all walks of life—homekeepers, office managers, ministers, line managers, counselors, and senior executives, to name a few.

We are confident in this material and have seen all the types respond well to the descriptors included here. We hope that understanding the source of the material and how it differs from many popular psychology books and other books on psychological type will help you become a more discerning consumer as well as give you the freedom to enjoy this work without having doubts about its validity.

Here is what you can look forward to in the chapters ahead. Chapter 1 describes Jung and Myers' models and discusses the theoretical assumptions about type. Chapter 2 explores important type preferences and type dynamic behaviors that have a data-rich basis. Chapter 3 explores deeper layers of type interactions and looks at how some of those interactions are expressed in behaviors that can fool casual type watchers. Chapter 4 reviews a special issue in psychological type, the inferior function. Chapter 5 examines issues of adult development and guidance that type development has to offer as we mature. Chapter 6 discusses the implications of type in our pathways of communication. The issue of valuing differences is examined in chapter 7, with detailed examples of how the types are likely to experience and express valuing. Chapter 8 offers our conclusion and comments on the next evolution of psychological type.

The book's postscript is written with practitioners in mind; we hope it will illuminate the ethics involved in administering and interpreting the MBTI, with particular emphasis on the moral problems created when using psychological type. If you are currently administering or interpreting the MBTI and/or contracting for those services from an external vendor, this chapter will be critical to your handling of those endeavors.

So, who is "normal"? In large measure, we all are. Our hope is that in these pages you will find the insights into yourself and others that will provide you with the courage to celebrate, in all its many forms, the normalcy of us all.

Acknowledgments

We gratefully acknowledge the support and encouragement of our spouses, Angela and Tom. They have shared our joys and frustrations throughout the process of distilling the passions into ideas, researching material, developing workshops, and the writing of this book. We also express thanks to Elizabeth Cottrell for sharing the gifts of her eyes, heart, and mind as she critiqued the manuscript. We are indebted for the seminal work of Isabel Myers and Mary McCaulley, and we feel priviledged to extend their work. We could not begin to list the hundreds of individuals who have given their insights and have given permission to use their reactions to our material; we appreciate their contributions. Finally, but not least, we are appreciative of the staff of Davies-Black Publishing for their labor in bringing this work into existence for the general public.

HABITS OF MIND

Jung and Psychological Type

*A*t first waking in early dawn, we may be faintly aware of birds singing, cars moving down the road, the feeling of an empty stomach. As we move toward greater consciousness, the sensations slowly intensify toward a complete and poignant awareness of being alive. Images from the previous night's dreams may float through the mind; we may make some effort to give meaning or bring order to the story. Slowly, recognition of the full day ahead brings us to attention and makes us climb out of bed. For some, these early moments of awareness are replete with wave after wave of physical sensation: the sunlight on the curtains, the coolness of that certain spot on the sheets that hasn't been occupied for a while. Others may be more aware of an inner voice planning the day and reviewing the possibilities it holds. Some may decide what things are most important to do today; a few will even announce, whether or not anyone is around to hear it, "My to-do's today include. . . ." By the time we sit down for breakfast, our direction of awareness and attention has already provided clues about our habits.

This direction of awareness, the selectivity of attention, and the focus of the mind's eye from the earliest moments of morning to the final instant of consciousness before sleep at night make up an individual's psychological type. Carl G. Jung's concept of a psychological type is, at its heart, an examination of the way we attend to, bring order to, and make decisions about our awareness.[1] Some psychologists have suggested that our perceptions are the realities about which we make judgments and take actions. If this is true, understanding the mechanisms by which we formulate our perceptions becomes critical to understanding our habitual behavior. If personality type theory is real, as we believe it is, habits of behavior are the expressions of typical patterns of perception and judgment embedded in each person's consciousness.

For example, a person who habitually focuses on the details of the world around her will likely exhibit behaviors concerned with precision, accuracy, and the order of details in the present moment. Likewise, if a person experiences life more like an impressionist painting, seeing few clear details but gaining a vivid image of the overall scene, we might hypothesize that his behaviors are likely to be concerned with patterns, possibilities, and nurturing an emerging vision to be fully expressed in the future. These are but two examples of the variety of interplay between habits of mind and observable behavior.

Psychological Type in Context of Individual Personality

While hypotheses about personality can be based upon distinct and observable patterns, using personality type to predict behavior is unwise; there are myriad other influences on behavior. Jung conceived of personality type as a habit of mind, not a fixed and unbreakable pattern, and his use of *type* was really shorthand for *typical*. American translations and current usage of *type* tend to imply *typecast* or *stereotype*, but this connotation was the farthest thing from the mind of Jung, and from the minds of Katharine Briggs and Isabel Briggs Myers when they actualized Jung's theory in the *Myers-Briggs Type Indicator* personality inventory.[2]

We know, of course, that while we tend to be most comfortable with our habits, they do not always dictate or predict our behavior or responses. And so it is with our psychological type, or habit of mind. While the patterns of an individual's direction and process of attention are shared by others, each individual has a unique personal psychology and behaves in ways that may have other roots.

People's life experiences, the demands of their current situation, their developmental stage in life (the perspective of adulthood is a good deal richer than the one of childhood), and other inborn dispositions such as intelligence are all behavior-influencing factors in addition to psychological type. For example, if a natural extravert who gets energy from interacting with others is raised in an abusive home, he may learn that thinking out loud leads to conflict. As an adult, he may revert to a silent thought process or detached coping strategy when he feels threatened or stressed. A woman's biological clock or a man's midlife crisis may beget all kinds of behavior that are not expressions of natural type preferences. But their behavior and emotions are real nonetheless. This is precisely why we cannot make predictions of behavior or competencies based solely upon a person's type preferences. Much to the chagrin of many type enthusiasts, we must say loudly: Type does not explain everything!

Yet to deny that we have habits is to ignore that we generally hold our forks the same way at every meal, that we usually put on our clothes in the same order, shave our legs or faces in the same pattern, react to questions with much the same facial expressions, and respond to certain stimuli consistently the same way. These habits of being pervade our thoughts and external behaviors. They do not, however, preclude or exclude other responses. When the situation calls for it, a healthy individual can adapt, breaking old habits and rising to the occasion. So the words *typical* and *habitual*, when applied to a person, do not mean that the person is rigid, fixed, or exclusive, but they do give some image, some sense of the individual's patterns of seeing and responding to the world.

Amid the richness of experiences and situational demands, defined and discernible patterns of perceiving and judging information can still be reasonably understood. Lest anyone feel that applying personal traits to a pattern somehow compromises individuality, note that even fingerprints, the most renowned and overused metaphor of personal uniqueness, can be sorted into categories of recognizable patterns (the FBI, for example, sorts them into four classifications for faster identification—loops, arcs, whorls, and accidental lines). So too does psychological type provide a pattern or structure onto which our unique and individual experiences and mind-sets are grafted. With the understanding that it is but one of many influences on behavior, let us now turn our full attention to understanding psychological type.

An Overview of the Model

In his book *Psychological Types,* Swiss psychologist Carl G. Jung suggested that we can sort typical mental habits among opposite poles of three personality dimensions.[3] The first and perhaps most pervasive dimension pertains to the primary source and direction of a person's energy. According to Jung's theory, the primary direction of psychological energy is focused toward either the outer world or the inner world. Jung used the terms *extraversion* and *introversion* to describe this distribution of energy. The second dimension, which he referred to as a mental or cognitive function, has to do with how we perceive information and what kind of information is initially attractive to us. The two poles of this dimension are *sensing*, a preference for sensory data that we recognize via our five senses, and *intuition*, a preference for relational, abstract data that we recognize via our intuition. Jung's third dimension, also referred to as a mental or cognitive function, pertains to our typical patterns for making decisions or judgments about the information we have perceived. One pattern, *thinking*, involves decisions based on interest in and attention to an object with cause-and-effect analysis. The other pattern, *feeling*, involves equally rational decisions based on personal values and relational impact.

The American mother-and-daughter team of Katharine Briggs and Isabel Briggs Myers contributed to Jung's schema by adding a fourth polar dimension. It focuses on habits of external orientation either toward orderliness and decisiveness, called *judgment*, or toward new information and "going with the flow," called *perception*. They named these poles after the mental function to which they are related. As you will see, the judgment orientation is associated with the judging mental functions (Thinking and Feeling). Likewise, the perceiving orientation is associated with the perceiving mental functions (Sensing and Intuition). This fourth dimension allows for quick identification of typical extraverted expressions in all people;[4] it will be covered in detail later. The four polar dimensions of Extraversion (E) and Introversion (I), Sensing (S) and Intuition (N), Thinking (T) and Feeling (F), and Judging (J) and Perceiving (P) presented by Jung, Myers, and Briggs make up a psychological typology, a set of typical habits of mind.

Jung spent the majority of his book *Psychological Types* discussing his anthropological observations of a wide variety of cultures. He pondered how human beings from incredibly different cultures could share basic qualities and yet be so different. From his studies he proposed that the world is made up of polarities. His source for the theory is the presence of polarities in the symbols found in all cultures. These range from the common—night and day, male and female, foreground and background, wet and dry— to the more philosophical, such as yin and yang, life and death, heaven and hell. Jung's point was that for a concept like heaven to have any substantial meaning, there has to be a contrasting concept of hell. He went on to propose that the psyche is also bounded by polarities, and wrote about the polarities of consciousness and unconsciousness as well as, most notably, extraversion and introversion. The psychological polarities Jung proposed are no different from the other polarities he observed and documented: We can and do utilize both poles of each dimension, but only in sequence, not simultaneously.[5] This is why the dimensions of this model are not set on a continuum and why the questions on the MBTI instrument force a choice between two options. A continuum implies a simultaneous, measurable utilization of the opposites in some percentage format; Jung's model is based on the reality that one cannot focus perfectly on details and on generalities *at the same instant*. An individual can, and most do, have access to and exhibit skills associated with each of the poles, depending on the situation. But we cannot access them concurrently. The question is not "Which one do I do?" but rather "Which do I do first?" or "Which is most comfortable or reliable?" It is extremely important to realize that the presence of polarities and the reality of an individual's pull toward a pole does not imply an either/or situation. You are not entirely either an extravert or an introvert. Healthy, normal individuals have and use both poles, but they do have a preference for one over the other. Jung proposed that this is also true for both of the mental or cognitive functions included in his typology, and Myers argued similarly about orientations to the outer world when she added it as a fourth dimension in the MBTI.[6]

The Model in Context:
Ancient Traditions of Personality Observations

Jung and Myers were not the first to observe personality types, nor was Jung the first to write about a typology of awareness. One of the oldest such typologies is part of the American Plains Indian tradition of the medicine wheel,[7] which assumes that each individual comes into the world with a way of perception that is but a beginning point in understanding others and the world. To these people, one's task in life is to master not only one's own way of perception but each of the others. To put it briefly, this model holds that each person is born into a particular way of seeing the world: the buffalo way, logical and analytical; the eagle way, seeing patterns and flying high above the details; the bear way, relational and connected to the environment; or the mouse way, grounded and close to the roots and details of life. The addition of various colors and directions to these basic descriptions (a person might be signified as a green bear looking inward, for example) honored the complexity and uniqueness of the individual while showing the patterns common to all people. Tribal elders identified the way of a child after much careful observation. As tribe members demonstrated mastery in looking at and appreciating other people's ways, the elders granted stones to them for placement on symbolic medicine wheels. An individual's wheel was then carried in such a way that those approaching could see from the number and placement of stones on his shield or her buckle how accomplished that person was in seeing other people's points of view. These Indians saw their life work as achieving movement around the medicine wheel to become expert at all views of life. This simple but elegant system was a model of the human psyche, and it informs us that type is a very old system with ancient roots in cultural understanding of processes. Myers and Jung provide continuity to this tradition with their contemporary revision of the theory.

The Framework

Psychological type suggests that there is a pattern within each of us by which we engage with, perceive, and act on the world. This pattern can be determined by pondering the extent to which we are pulled toward one or the other pole of each of four dimensions:

(E)	Extraverting	**ENERGY**	Introverting	**(I)**
(S)	Sensing	**PERCEPTION**	Intuiting	**(N)**
(T)	Thinking	**JUDGMENT**	Feeling	**(F)**
(J)	Judging	**ORIENTATION**	Perceiving	**(P)**

We will review, in depth, each of the dimensions in the model, for it is vital to understand these polarities in order to be able to cross the threshold leading to the heart of the type. Ultimately, personality type is about the dynamic within a person's habits of mind that lead to typical behavioral expressions. The dynamic is understood in terms of how these dimensions relate to each other to create a sum that is truly greater than its individual parts.

The Model in Depth:
Finding Your Own Home Bases

To find individual preferences, it helps to describe the two poles of each dimension and determine which has the stronger pull.

Sorting Among Extraversion and Introversion

Your type preferences are on automatic pilot during every waking hour. They balance your external management of situations with internal pushes and pulls that motivate you. To Jung, extraversion and introversion were more than differences of social acuity; they create an energy field. Extraverts are stimulus hungry.[8] Extraverted minds seek external activity, change, and interaction to create the energy needed to guide the self through the day. But note well that within the person with an Extraverted preference, even while the Extraversion is active and the person is aware of this need for stimulation, Introversion is still at work outside of awareness. Within any person, it is never a situation of having access to the poles of the dimensions in an "either-or" fashion, but rather it should be considered in terms of "preference, and . . . ." One's preference for Extraversion is always aided by Introverted energy processes, though those processes are typically outside of ready awareness. The reverse is also true for the person with a preference for Introversion, whose awareness is likely to be focused on the inner world of thoughts and ideas even while navigating grocery aisles and boardrooms.

Jung referred to the extraverted and introverted processes as attitudes, and we will use his language to refer to them throughout our work. For many people reading Jung's work today, *attitude*, when used to refer to the processes of extraversion and introversion, causes a bit of confusion. We have come to use the word today to refer to a person's motivation level. But when Jung was translated to English in the 1920s, the word *attitude* had much more to do with physical positioning than with a state of mind. If you look at some of the murder mysteries written during the period, you will see the word used like so: "The attitude of the body was face down with the left arm extended to the side." In talking about extraversion and introversion, Jung was concerned with the physical direction of the mind's eye. For a given individual, it is directed either mostly externally, seeking to exert and collect its energy from the world outside (Extraversion), or internally, focusing on and drawing sustenance from a vivid and rich inner world of thoughts and ideas (Introversion). Though assuming that we all use both energy sources, Jung theorized that any individual prefers one source over the other, much as one prefers left-handedness or right-handedness.

This balancing of energy is of practical significance. The person who prefers Extraversion is responding externally, seeking an event to be experienced. So strong is this impulse that the Extravert may talk out loud, even when alone, in order to experience an external event and make his thoughts real. All the while his Introverted process is internalizing that experience, seeking to make sense of all that is happening externally. Without the functioning of Introversion, the Extravert babbles like a shallow brook soon to be evaporated by the heat of living.

The individual who prefers Introversion is aware of the internal world of experiences and is generally less in tune with the Extraverted energy field. The Introvert uses Extraverted functioning as a practical way of getting from the sofa to the bathroom in an unfamiliar home, or finding the correct gate in a busy airport. But the trip provides no source of stimulation, and once arrived at the destination, the Introvert may wonder what route she took to get there. An Introvert without the functioning of Extraversion simulates a catatonic state of being.

Sometimes children give us the most natural and expressive examples of type in action. We, the authors, are inveterate observers of children, our own and others, and we will offer stories of them throughout to illustrate our points. And while we recognize that type is not the only force at work in these interactions, sometimes the type influence is so clear that we have to laugh out loud. A story from each of our households illustrates what can go on when Introverts and Extraverts get together.

Olivia and Luke Pearman are two years apart in age. Luke clearly prefers Extraversion and Olivia, the elder, prefers Introversion. Once, at the ages of about four and six, they were in the car and Luke was giving a running commentary on all that he saw around him. "There's a red car . . . the radio is playing a good song . . . there's a McDonalds, I'm hungry. . . ." After a few minutes, Olivia burst out, "Luke! It is what it is; now just shut up!" Luke immediately responded, "I can't shut up, Olivia. My brain keeps telling me things and I don't know how to turn it off!"

Sarah's husband Tom has a clear preference for Extraversion, while her son Wells seems to prefer Introversion. It is not unusual for Tom to be talking to Wells about something at length and for Wells to finally ask, "Daddy, who are you talking to?"—he'd tuned out all the "noise" many minutes before. One day on the way to kindergarten Tom was going on about something and Wells asked, "Daddy, WHAT are you talking about?" Tom, who knows a good deal about type, said, "Son, I was just thinking out loud. Sometimes I talk about things in order to understand them. Don't you ever do that?" Wells laughed as if he had caught Tom trying to pull a joke on him and replied, "No, Daddy, I don't. That's backwards."

In the business environment, Extraversion and Introversion can provide no end of misunderstanding. What to an Extraverted supervisor is a lively brainstorming session can sound to an Introverted employee like a list of tasks for the upcoming quarter. We have heard many stories of team meetings in which Extraverts begin with one set of ideas about a problem and through lengthy discussion reach a conclusion entirely different from the starting point. This can confuse the Introverts, causing them to wonder which ideas to actually act upon—the initial plans or the later ones. An hour after the meeting, some of the Introverts may have another series of suggestions which, offered at that point, can be interpreted by the Extraverts as counterproductive—"Why didn't you just say so an hour ago? We already reached our conclusions. Now we have to get everybody together again to talk about it!" And so the circle dance can continue *ad infinitum* (or *ad nauseam*, depending on your viewpoint!).

This distinction between Extraversion and Introversion is profound but greatly misunderstood. People who have seriously reflected on their observations of life cannot reasonably question that the distinction exists, and no personality researcher in the last forty years has had serious doubts about the presence of Extraversion and Introversion in humans. But the Americanized version of Jung's formulation has led to the false conclusion that Extraversion means outgoing and gregarious behavior, and that Introversion means shyness and withdrawn behavior.[9] The kernel of truth is that Extraversion seeks to initiate and Introversion is inclined to receive and reflect. Shyness, however, is a function of anxiety when in the presence of other people, and it occurs regardless of a preference for Introversion or Extraversion. It is more probably related to early childhood experiences. Likewise, gregariousness is also largely a function of expectation and training and occurs in Introverts and Extraverts alike.

In typology, in these habits of mind, Extraversion and Introversion are processes of charging our mental batteries. Some are aware of, and act upon, a need to initiate—to seek stimulus. Others are aware of a need for the energy that comes from reflection. Whichever is the main source of awareness, the opposite process fulfills needs that are beyond awareness.

The Extravert's relationship with the environment serves an important purpose. By definition, Extraversion means seeking energy from the world outside the self; thus Extraverts report feeling a real need to "think out loud." In other words, externalized thought takes on a richer, more complex meaning for the Extravert.

Thoughts forced to stay inside may be experienced like the white noise of a radio tuned between channels where the frequency is sporadic. Sometimes the thought or idea only begins to make sense, the frequency only comes in clear and strong, after it has been brought outside the self. But the underlying goal of the initiation is to seek out and collect energy from outside the self.

The Introvert, on the other hand, is less likely to feel the need to externalize thoughts or ideas until the pressure to communicate with others requires it. Like a Japanese garden that offers new views as a person walks through it, the Introvert's new experiences or ideas are satisfying in and of themselves; energy comes through the peace and elegance of the internal garden rather than from outside stimuli. Extraversion initiates in the environment; Introversion is initiated within a person and spends its energy by painting an internal picture of what is real.

Extraversion and Introversion are as different to people as batteries and software are to a laptop computer: Each is essential but they serve different purposes. The attitudes of Extraversion and Introversion, as psychological types, are the processes that create the energy field each person has with the world. This energy exchange can be represented in the following way:

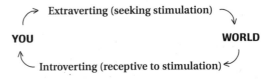

If you are new to personality type, take a moment to ask yourself, "Where do I get my batteries charged most frequently?" Do you get "juice" externally, by initiating, in which case your primary pull or preference may be for Extraversion? Or are you revitalized internally, by receiving and reflecting, in which case your preference may be for Introversion. Remember that you are doing both. But which is easiest and most energizing for you? Of which process are you most aware? Make a note in the margin of this page—*E* if you suspect you prefer Extraversion, *I* if you think you prefer Introversion.

Sorting Among Sensing and Intuition

We have described Extraversion and Introversion as basic energy exchange processes. Taking in information and making decisions about information—perception and judgment—are core human mental functions. The perceptual dimension in type—that is, how we take in or perceive information—revolves around tendencies toward either specific and factual existence or theoretical and global existence.

Some of us are pulled toward concrete, matter-of-fact information that we experience directly and exactly. This pull to the pragmatic and realistic matters of life is referred to as Sensing perception. Individuals with the Sensing preference are drawn to facts like metal to magnets; they feel an urge for clarity and prefer that the matters they deal with be of practical importance. These individuals often express their creativity by adapting familiar strategies to solve newly presented problems. This is the type of creativity displayed when Edison tried out hundreds of possibilities before finding a workable light bulb filament: consistent adaptation of the known. People with a Sensing preference are thus often experienced by others as methodical, certain, adamant about details, and focused on the here and now.

Those who are pulled to the figurative, to ideas and various associations of possibilities, are said to have an Intuitive perceiving preference. Rather than feeling the urge for clarity, people preferring Intuition have an urge to acquire knowledge and to seek complexity in information. The Intuitive perception trusts ideas like the eyes trust light. The striving for the association of ideas is often so strong that, like two sticks rubbing together to create fire, Intuition creates innovation. People with the Intuitive preference are thus often seen by others as imaginative, unconventional, intellectual, and having a mental focus on the future.

These qualitatively different perceptual pulls lead to profound differences of expression in communications. Often those with a Sensing preference are drawn to the specificity, details, and action plan portions of a project; those with an Intuitive preference are more likely to be drawn to the goals, models, and ideas framing the project. Without an awareness of these differing tendencies, the Sensing type might see the Intuitive type's reliance on models and theories as a person with his or her "head in the clouds," and the Intuitive type might see the Sensing type's interest in details and practicalities as being "a stick-in-the-mud." But a little reflection makes it clear that both types are needed to complete most complex projects, because the idea behind a project is as important as the details of the plan that implements it—one cannot exist without the other!

The same is true within an individual. A person whose primary pull is toward Sensing may often have hunches and a vision for the future, but is more likely to spend energy talking about or exploring practical applications of an idea and may not act until the verifying data are in place. An individual pulled toward Intuitive processes is aware of details, but is likely to put those details into a larger context in order to make meaning of them, perhaps talking about or exploring various abstract relationships between today's choices and choices that may crop up tomorrow.

These differences are profound and difficult to describe. Jung referred to the perceiving function as *irrational*,[10] but *nonrational* probably works better in our current usage. Think about it. How do you come to know things? If we do base decisions on our perceptions of events, understanding where our perceptions originate is vital, and yet the search is as for figures in the mist. Another teaching story from our children may illustrate both the dynamic tension between these modes of perception and the innate nature of the process.

Roger's son, Luke, and Sarah's son, Wells, have been best buddies from the start; they are very close in age. We suspect that Luke gets his information from his senses, while Wells seems to be more tuned to intuitive messages. One beautiful day when they were around four years old, they were outside swinging together, side by side. Luke was joyously exclaiming and reporting about all his sensory experiences: "The breeze is in my hair and feels cool! The sky is blue and so is that toy train and so are my pants! The grass is green and tickles my feet! The trees are green, too!" Wells, not to be outdone, shouted, "The trees are pushing the sky!" Luke's rejoinder was the sort many people preferring Intuition feel they get from pragmatists. He said, "No, they're not."

No one told the children what to pay attention to or how they should experience that glorious afternoon. The verbal expressions they chose were absolutely natural. There they were, not ten inches from each other, both swinging, both facing the same direction, for all intents and purposes having the same physical experience, and yet their perceptions of it were so radically different. How do we know what we know? It is difficult to tease it apart, and yet the pattern of difference between Sensing knowledge and Intuitive knowledge is undeniable.

For example, during an intense discussion by the members of a Research and Development Task Force for a financial company, those relying on Sensing kept pushing to use historical trends and specific data sources as benchmarks, but those with Intuitive preferences wondered aloud if the group was too buried in the past. Clearly both sides had important points to make. It is interesting, though, how during moments of stress we tend to exaggerate our typical responses and ignore other kinds of information. Professional observers of such situations often note these exaggerated states as people with opposing preferences play out their differences.

Here is another spot to stop and contemplate your own patterns of perception. Are you pulled more to the traditions, hard data, and sensory realities of life, or more to visions of the future that are guided by models and theories and ideas? Again, make a note in the margin of this page before going on, *S* for Sensing or *N* for Intuition (as *I* denotes Introversion, *N* is used as shorthand for Intuition).

Sorting Among Thinking and Feeling

Taking in information, as we all do through our Sensing and Intuitive functions, is but one part of the natural processing of information. Healthy individuals are also driven to decide on the merit or worth of the information after it has been taken in. A plenitude of studies have shown the human tendency toward judgment. We are wired to make meaning out of information, to decide on its relative importance, its sensibility, and how it fits into our world views.[11] Jung suggested that we are pulled toward either an analytical, cause-and-effect type of judgment (thinking) or a value-oriented, accommodating type of judgment (feeling). Jung and Myers were quick to point out that both thinking and feeling are subjective and rational functions, but that the former places importance on the subjective experience of logic whereas the latter places importance on the subjective experience of how likes and dislikes affect outcomes. Jung wrote that thinking types experience the world as an object, feeling types as a subject.[12] In other words, those with the habit of initially stepping out of a situation and looking at the variables see the world as an object; those who look at the relations involved and step into a situation to attend to its effects on others see the world as a subject. The initial decision to step into or out of a new situation depends on what subjects hold the individual's interest and attention.

Individuals who are pulled toward Thinking judgments are often seen as critical (thus less accepting), logical, and questioning. When assessing any situation, their likely first sequence of thought is: "if A, then B. . . ." The urge to verify information, to explore independent sources of information, and to insist on sequential reasoning is, for those with a Thinking preference, as natural as a river running downhill. The Thinking judgment function is directed toward a particular outcome, moves with great momentum, and follows an orderly route to its destination.

Those with a preference for Feeling judgments are often seen as accepting, trusting of emotions, fair-minded, and seeking of consensus. The urge is toward consistency with personal values rather than the apparent principles or logic of a situation. The first tendency is to examine how information and outcomes affect individuals. Feeling types may describe their acute awareness of the intricacies of a network as a delicate web that connects us all, such that movement anywhere on the web can be felt throughout the web, not just in the immediate area. Their thinking about a new situation is not likely to be "if A, then B," but rather "if A, then B, D, N, and Q, and that's just for starters." Feeling types respond first with acceptance of an individual and a desire to accommodate before bringing logic and analysis to a situation. Two examples illustrate how Thinking and Feeling often play out. One is from the business world, the other from a professional society.

During consultation with a manufacturing company, a vice president expressed great disappointment that the company was about to lose a very effective plant manager. The vice president had puzzled over the situation and was unable to see how to prevent the loss. By his account, this manager had gotten superior raises and other financial benefits, and was consistently given high marks on his annual review, which went into his personnel file. Asked to assess the situation and to intervene or at least clarify the reasons for the valued employee's departure, the consultant interviewed the manager. In that conversation the manager said things like, "I work hard for this company and get no appreciation. I can work anywhere for the money. I want to work where people really appreciate what I do—where I'll know that it matters that *I* come in to work, not just any plant manager with my expertise." Upon hearing this, the baffled vice president said again, "But we've given him raises! Stock! We point out all of his abilities during annual reviews! How can he not feel appreciated?" Simply put, the vice president had a Thinking preference and the manager had a Feeling preference. For the Feeling type, competency is basically assumed and regular expressions of appreciation are needed; for the Thinking type, appreciation is basically assumed and need only be confirmed by regular pay raises and/or increases in responsibility. Obviously the two have very different definitions of the word *appreciation*. This example came from one company, but we have heard virtually the same words from employees in at least three other manufacturing companies.

The other example comes from the board of a very small volunteer nonprofit organization. The board signed a contract with a speaker to present a workshop; it stated that after all the bills for the event had been paid, the speaker would receive a high percentage of the remainder. The speaker was a longtime friend to the organization and hoped the event would succeed so that the group would have some cash flow for future programs. The event was indeed a great success with lots of attendees. Six weeks later the treasurer of the organization reasoned that all the bills had been submitted, so he totaled up the figures and wrote the speaker a check for the appropriate percentage of the money left over. But three days after the check was sent out, another sizable and legitimate bill was submitted. "What should I do?" thought the treasurer. This bill significantly decreased the profits from the event, and therefore the speaker had been vastly overpaid within the context of the contract. To the treasurer, the proper action was clear: call the speaker and explain the circumstances. Especially since the speaker was a friend and wanted the program to enlarge the coffers of the organization, the payment would simply be renegotiated in light of the new information. No big deal.

But this board knew something about type. The treasurer knew he was the only person on the board with a preference for making Thinking judgments, and that all the others preferred Feeling. So, he thought, "It seems clear to me what to do, but I know others may have a different view. I'll ask the rest of the board what they want me to do." That's when the real learning began. To the persons with a Feeling preference, the decision was equally clear— eat the loss. Their rational response was that this small organization depends on the good will of speakers in the area to virtually donate their time to present programs. Even with a successful program, the amount they paid the speaker was barely a pittance. To ask for a renegotiation of fees at this time would seriously damage the integrity of the organization and the network upon which it relies. From the board's perspective, it would be irresponsible to jeopardize the organization's ability to serve its members in the future because of a bookkeeping error. Thus, there were two radically different ways of approaching the same problem. The real gift of understanding type is the knowledge that there might be different but equally valid views about an issue, and that discussion about these views need not dissolve into an unpleasant personal argument.

Of all the psychological type dimensions, the distinction between Thinking and Feeling brings the most debate. Culture generally values and teaches logical, linear, and analytical problem solving. It is often difficult at first for those whose true preference is for Feeling to separate it from such cultural conditioning. As consultants, we have seen over and over again in our work with major corporations the blind spot caused by overreliance on the Thinking attributes. We have often asked corporate workers to respond anonymously to this query: "Visualize this organization five years from now after it has developed self-directed teams (or whatever phrase the company uses for fully functioning teams). As you imagine your successful team, describe the characteristics that make it effective. What are you doing that helps you achieve the success you want?" Consistently the overwhelming responses are: "We listen thoroughly to each other." "Different views are tolerated and encouraged." "We care about each other." "We can take a risk without fear of reprisal."[13] This may explain why the shelves of major chain bookstores display such titles as *Emotional Intelligence, Care of the Soul, Servant Leadership,* and *Habits of Heart,* all of which tap into the need for balance in the workplace between these two equally rational ways of making judgments.

Interestingly but perhaps not surprisingly, this is the only type dimension on which we see gender differences in the general population. On the MBTI, a majority of women say they have a preference for Feeling, and a majority of men report themselves as having a preference for Thinking.[14] Much of the work that you see today on gender differences also describes quite accurately the differences between Thinking and Feeling judgments, regardless of the gender of the person with the preference.

Some believe there is a kind of parallel development of these two processes. Our experience is that individuals have real, basic preferences that rely first on either personal logic or on personal values.

Pause here again for reflection on your preferred method of making decisions. Mark *T* in the margin of this page if you have a preference for Thinking, or *F* if your preference is for Feeling.

Myers' Innovation: Sorting Among Perception and Judgment

Myers agreed with Jung's notion that both the public self (extraverted energy) and the private self (introverted energy) combine with the mental functions of perception and judgment to create a complex system. She set out to simplify it by developing a way of examining typical extraverted and introverted mental functions through the use of a construct she called orientation to the outer world. Her suggestion was that the behavior and habits of the public (extraverted) self give a strong clue about the dynamic of the individual's complete type orientation. She hypothesized that the poles of outward orientation could be recognized by decisive, orderly, and planned expression, or by ad hoc, casual, and spontaneous expression. The former she referred to as *judgment*, the latter as *perception*.[15] By giving these the same names as the poles of the mental functions, she inferred that orientation preference, regardless of attitude preference, predicts whether a person's judgment processes (Thinking or Feeling) or perceiving processes (Sensing or Intuition) are typically in the extraverted mode. The alternate mental function, then, would typically operate in the introverted attitude. In other words, if you extravert judgment, then you introvert perception; if you extravert perception, then you introvert judgment.

People with a preference for the Judging orientation are likely to express satisfaction with getting a job completed well before a deadline. They are driven to make decisions, to bring closure to things in the external world. While they are fully capable of handling last-minute changes and chaos, the voice in their head is likely to be saying, "If I had planned better, this wouldn't have happened. What can I learn from this to make sure it doesn't happen again?" These folks are likely to be very attached to their calendars and goal sheets and are often quite skilled at prioritizing the tasks necessary to meet a goal. Their to-do lists will almost certainly feature discernible orders of priority. The downside is a tendency to become attached to a particular outcome, rather than remaining open to new information that might lead to a better outcome. Still, the need for completion can work wonders when the going gets tough, and the proclivity for action can be crucial in today's fast-paced environment.

The person with a preference for the Perceiving orientation is pulled, in the external world, to remain open to new information, to go with the flow. Whereas people who prefer Judging might nag themselves to plan things better, the Perceiving type, though able to make and follow a detailed plan, may wonder, "If I plan or decide this now, will I be able to respond if something better comes along, or if I receive more information later?" Note, however, that research shows that actual procrastination seems to cut across both types.[16] In general, folks with a preference for Perceiving appear to the world to be fairly laid back, unconcerned with the exact schedule of events because they are confident that the process will lead to the best outcome, whatever it may be. As a result, folks with a Perceiving preference are often very comfortable with ambiguity and last-minute changes. The downside of this pull is remaining open too long and missing opportunities for action. The benefit is that people with this preference are often more open to unexpected outcomes and may be able to find success where others would see failure.

Moments before Sarah and Tom were to be married, one of the bridesmaids rushed up to Sarah and said, "We are one bouquet short! I have no flowers!" Simultaneously a groomsman approached and said, "We are one boutonniere short, too!" Rather than seeing this as a failure and feeling that all her hopes for a perfect wedding were dashed, Sarah calmly assessed her resources and then took a bouquet from the maid of honor and another from her sister, the matron of honor. One of the bouquets she gave to the empty-handed bridesmaid; the other she quickly disassembled, handing a single lily to the maid, one to the matron, and creating a boutonniere from the remainder for the groomsman. The wedding went off on time, and because Sarah's mother grows prize-winning lilies, everyone in the church thought that the maid and matron of honor carrying a single perfect lily was a purposeful decision. For years after in that community, it was *de rigueur* for the maids of honor to carry a single stem flower rather than a full bouquet. Remaining open to outcomes saved the day in that case. (Skeptics may rightly say that if Sarah had just counted the flowers earlier the whole crisis might have been avoided! Still, the unexpected outcome was a lovely new tradition that added something to their ceremony and to many others.)

You know what to do at this point. In which direction do you think you are pulled most in your dealings with the outer world? Do people around you see and hear you making decisions and judgments, reaching closure about the events in your life, or do they see you maintaining an air of flexibility and openness to whatever may come? Note a *J* in the margin if you think you prefer a Judging orientation, or *P* if you're more inclined to the Perceiving orientation.

Now thumb back through this chapter and find your margin notes; there should be four. Together they look something like ESTJ or INFP or ENTP or ISFJ. There are sixteen possibilities (by convention, the four letters are listed in the following order: E or I; S or N; T or F; J or P). This is your personality profile, but for now consider it to be only a rough-cut hypothesis. Be open to changing your mind about it as you move through the rest of the book.

TABLE 1

EXTRAVERTED AND INTROVERTED MENTAL FUNCTIONS

Self-Sort Profile				Extraverted Mental Function as Determined from Orientation Preference (J or P)	Introverted Mental Function
Energy	*Perception*	*Judgment*	*Orientation*		
I	S	T	J	Thinking (T)	Sensing (S)
I	N	T	J	Thinking (T)	Intuition (N)
E	S	T	J	Thinking (T)	Sensing (S)
E	N	T	J	Thinking (T)	Intuition (N)
I	S	F	J	Feeling (F)	Sensing (S)
I	N	F	J	Feeling (F)	Intuition (N)
E	S	F	J	Feeling (F)	Sensing (S)
E	N	F	J	Feeling (F)	Intuition (N)
I	S	T	P	Sensing (S)	Thinking (T)
I	S	F	P	Sensing (S)	Feeling (F)
E	S	T	P	Sensing (S)	Thinking (T)
E	S	F	P	Sensing (S)	Feeling (F)
I	N	T	P	Intuition (N)	Thinking (T)
I	N	F	P	Intuition (N)	Feeling (F)
E	N	T	P	Intuition (N)	Thinking (T)
E	N	F	P	Intuition (N)	Feeling (F)

Note: This table will be referred to many times, so study it and make a note of this page number for future reference.

The self-sorting on the *Myers-Briggs Type Indicator* personality inventory produces a shorthand four-letter code that yields the system shown in table 1.[17]

We will use the vocabulary from table 1 regularly throughout the work, especially in the next chapter. It will be well worth your time to really study this table and familiarize yourself with the language of, for example, Extraverted Thinking and Introverted Sensing, and how that relates to the Judging–Perceiving dimension. You may even want to dog-ear the table for quick reference later.

Research, both past and ongoing, shows that Jung and Myers were correct in their hypothesis that the sixteen types are measurably distinct from one another.[18] In following chapters you will read many descriptors of the different types as we, step by step, fully develop the picture that type can give us.

It is vitally important to remember here that for Jung and Myers these bipolar propositions assume that differences are valuable and constructive. Being different from others in one's perceptual or judgment patterns is neither good nor bad in and of itself, but *while all types are equally valuable, not all type expressions are equally valuable in all situations.* This differentiation between a person's type and typical expressions of type is one we will return to over and over throughout this work. Keep in mind that our goal in this endeavor is to understand the typical patterns, which may lead us to value human differences. We must not leap to the conclusion that this understanding is equal to valuing the rich differences that come from psychological types. Typology as a theory is straightforward, and it asserts that psychological type is a messy, sometimes chaotic dynamic that creates both clearly discernible patterns as well as tremendous variability in behavior. If personality type is used as a rigid, well-ordered system of defining, labeling, and predicting habits, it may be impossible to truly value differences. How can anyone value that which is stereotyped?

So far we have covered definitions of the basic scales within the model of personality type. If we left you here, you might think that each of these scales is a stand-alone piece such that your profile would read E,S,T,J or I,N,F,P. But this model really comes alive in what are called type dynamics. Type dynamics help to answer questions such as, "What happens when your preferences on the individual scales start interacting with one another?" "Is Extraverted Intuition different from Introverted Intuition?" "Why can't my spouse and I understand each other even though three of our four letters are the same?"

The evidence we will discuss in chapters 2 and 3 suggests that when Myers developed the J–P orientation scale she was on to more than just the orientations and their indication of extraverted mental functions. She actualized Jung's model by showing two things: first, that the extraverted and introverted functions work in tandem with each other, and second, that one or the other function pulls more urgently on an individual, with the remaining one serving a supportive role. Chapter 2 will offer you detailed information on those dynamics. Further, when she explored orientations, Myers tapped into issues such as how our upbringing affects our development, how we are motivated to work, and the nature of tolerance.

Jung and Myers gave us a way to understand differences in perception and judgment. While these preferences have observable behaviors that are markers of mental processes, they are far from being static or two-dimensional. As our senses of smell, taste, and sight commingle to create an experience, our type preferences synthesize with experience to create the personality we exhibit. This mental synthesis is known as type dynamics. Dynamics are as different from individual preferences as a free-standing three-dimensional figure is from a flat two-dimensional picture. How these dynamics and basic preferences interact is the subject of our next chapter.

A MESSY COMPLEXITY

The Patterns That Create Expressions of Heart

*I*f you had a choice between seeing Michelangelo's *David* in person or looking at a picture of that remarkable sculpture, chances are excellent that you would prefer to see the real thing. When showing our photo albums, we often feel compelled to tell a story or describe the person in the photograph in order to give a complete rendering of the picture. Should someone invite us to see a story through a slide show or the same story through a motion picture, we are likely to choose the motion picture. We all are partial to three-dimensional information. We want the motion, background, and simultaneous stimulation of sight, sound, and touch in order for the experience to feel real and be fully appreciated. We think of ourselves as complex individuals who cannot be adequately captured in just a snapshot—a videotape is likely to do a better job. In much the same way, learning about the eight dimensions of psychological type provides just a flat snapshot of the mental processes. Type dynamics, however, is the three-dimensional version; it is about the quality of who we are and the dramatic integration of all our capabilities to provide a response to the pressing needs of the moment. When, for example, within two minutes we can have a logical debate with a colleague and then give heartfelt sympathy to a friend who calls on the phone with sad news, we are showing our flexibility of response and utilization of different mental processes.

Mental Markers

Our mental processes work so fast and are so immediate that in each moment we process hundreds of thousands of pieces of information. Consequently, we must acknowledge that any aspect of psychological functioning is complex. We are left with looking at the behavioral markers that are the outcomes of these mental processes. An illustration of this richness and complexity is captured in *synesthesia*, the term biologists use to describe the phenomenon of the exponential effect of various senses interacting to create a whole awareness that one sense alone could never accomplish.[19] Stimulating one sense promotes a reaction by another sense. For example, when trying to create a luxurious dining experience, it is vital to know that, from a biological perspective, the visual presentation and the aroma of the food are just as important as the taste because the interaction of those factors produces a level of stimulation that one of the factors alone could never achieve. Auditory stimulation (Mozart versus honking traffic noise) would also have an impact on the total experience.

Preferences at Interplay

Likewise, in psychological type, the dynamic interplay and interaction of the preferences add to the richness of type. We must first understand, as Myers had proposed, that the preferences are distinct processes that work together to make up the whole, in much the same way that our senses are distinct but interact to create depth of experience.[20] Because of this interplay and complexity, it is unreasonable to declare that any given behavior of a person is caused by a single internal factor; it is more accurate to say that a behavior is an expression of interacting factors such as the attitudes of Extraversion or Introversion with one of the mental functions. And it is more true to say of people that their behavior at a given moment is an expression of what they are experiencing at that moment than to declare that they are behaving a particular way exclusively because of some trait or genetic quality.

As with our senses, each aspect of our psychological type serves an important function. Extraverted Sensing and Extraverted Intuition serve to give us different types of external perceptions. Introverted Sensing and Introverted Intuition provide a personal awareness of internal perceptions. Extraverted Thinking and Extraverted Feeling give us rational ways to respond and interact with others in the world. Introverted Thinking and Introverted Feeling inform our reflective and introspective judgments about experience. And as nature would have it, we all have developed particular strengths with each of these mental operations. Though we rely on all of them, they are not all equally expressive or apparent in our personalities. Understanding type dynamics gives us insight into the priority structure and nature of these mental processes in each one of us.

Through the exploration of the dynamics of type to follow, you will gain an awareness of the three-dimensional nature of psychological type. We hope this awareness will give us all a greater sensitivity to the complexity inherent in the mental processes suggested by type. Ultimately, we will have a practical way to understand differences in perception, communication, and action through learning about type dynamics. The dynamics of the type enable us to see the adaptation of the individual to specific situations and understand the resulting behavior.

Order of the Functions

Type theory says that because we cannot access all mental functions and attitudes at the same time, we use (and are aware of) mental functions in a particular order. The mental operation used most often and of which we are most aware is called the dominant function and attitude. The dominant function is always used in the preferred attitude. For example, the dominant function for those who prefer Introversion operates in the Introverted attitude; for those who prefer Extraversion, the dominant function operates in the Extraverted attitude. The dominant function for all types is superior in awareness, utility, and reliability, but not necessarily in the strength of its influence on our behaviors. A second mental operation, the auxiliary function, is frequently utilized and provides balance to the dominant, but operates slightly out of our awareness. If the dominant process is Extraverted, then the auxiliary function will be Introverted, and vice versa. A third function, called the tertiary, explains a variety of responses we make, on occasion, which are quite different from either our dominant or auxiliary processes. A fourth function, called the inferior, is infrequently used and, though very powerful, is often quite out of our awareness.

To be true to the whole theory, we must add that the four remaining function/attitude pairs (if your dominant is Extraverted Intuition, for example, Introverted Intuition would be one of these four) operate far away from awareness, deeply hidden in the unconscious, and are usually inaccessible to us through any direct route. Some believe these to be the aspects of dynamics that make up the nature of our "other self." The other self is that part of us that is the opposite in gender attributes. For example, the male

Extraverted Thinker who sometimes surprises even himself with tender, nurturing behavior may be expressing a Feeling function that resides deep in the feminine part of his psychology. Such matters are beyond the scope of this book. Suffice it to say that type theory suggests that deep within us we use all eight mental function/attitude pairs to serve conscious and unconscious purposes. Our goal here is to get a grasp on the use of the four primary mental functions, as these make up so much of our conscious awareness and choices.

Dominant and Auxiliary

Jung and Myers hypothesized that among a person's preferences is a dominant, or leading, mental process (Sensing, Intuition, Thinking, or Feeling) that is used in the preferred attitude (Extraversion or Introversion). They further theorized that there is an auxiliary or supporting mental process (again either Sensing, Intuition, Thinking, or Feeling) that is used in the nonpreferred attitude.[21] In table 1 at the end of the previous chapter, each type is listed with its Extraverted and Introverted mental functions. Look there and you can see that both ISTJ and ESTJ use Extraverted Thinking. For ESTJ, Extraverted Thinking is the dominant function; but for ISTJ Extraverted Thinking is the auxiliary function, while Introverted Sensing is the dominant function. Table 3 in this chapter lists the full dynamic order of awareness for each type. If you choose to use table 1, just remember that because the dominant function is always in the preferred attitude, for Introverted types the dominant function can be found in the Introverted mental function column, while for Extraverted types it can be found in the Extraverted mental function column.

An important point: Just as we cannot consciously extravert and introvert at the same time nor perceive with our senses and our intuition at the same time, we cannot both attend to information and decide on it at the same time; out of habit, one of the two will lead the way for the other.

The dominant process is the leader, the "captain of the ship," psychologically speaking.[22] It is the mental process of which we are most aware and on which we rely most heavily. In healthy individuals it is the most well-developed process, and nearly all type experts would agree it is the process that develops first in children. (It is especially difficult to determine the sequence and timing of type development with Introverted children, as they keep their dominant process to themselves!) For the majority of people, using the dominant process is very comfortable, efficient, and usually fairly effective.

The auxiliary process operates in support of the dominant process and, to our own awareness, usually behind the scenes. If, for example, a person's dominant function is a judging function (Thinking or Feeling), the auxiliary perceiving process (Sensing or Intuition) is busily feeding the judging process either ideas or data about which to make decisions. Conversely, if a person's dominant process is a perceiving process, the auxiliary judging process is in the background determining which of the many data or ideas are reasonable or valuable to pursue. We often are less aware of our auxiliary function at work, and yet it is always there. Sometimes this lesser awareness can lead us into misunderstandings.

Using the Secondary

When we interact with others using our auxiliary function, we may appear a bit blustery or evasive. Introverted Perceiving types (led by Introverted Sensing or Introverted Intuition) may be quite unaware of how critical or final their Extraverted judgments (Extraverted Thinking or Extraverted Feeling) seem to others. Extraverted Judging types may be equally unaware when their Introverted perceptions come across to others as noncommittal and confusing.

Let's look at a person whose preferences are for Extraversion with Sensing attention to details and who prefers to analyze those details in a Thinking way. In this case, Extraversion would combine with either Sensing or Thinking to become the dominant mental process, and the nonpreferred but still active Introversion would combine with the other function to serve as the auxiliary process. You can see now why Myers' addition of the J–P scale, indicating which function is used in the Extraverted mode, was so critical to a full understanding and identification of type dynamics. In this example, without knowing the person's preference for J or P, it would take many discussions to begin to identify which mental function serves as the dominant function. Myers' contribution was enormous.

Usage of the Four Functions

Remember, type theory holds that all four mental functions (Sensing, Intuition, Thinking, and Feeling) are always present but

TABLE 2

TRADITIONAL HIERARCHY OF TYPE DYNAMICS

EXTRAVERTED TYPES

	ESTJ	ENTJ	ESFJ	ENFJ	ESTP	ENTP	ESFP	ENFP
Lead	ET	ET	EF	EF	ES	EN	ES	EN
Auxiliary	IS	IN	IS	IN	IT	IT	IF	IF
Tertiary	IN	IS	IN	IS	IF	IF	IT	IT
Least Used	IF	IF	IT	IT	IN	IS	IN	IS

INTROVERTED TYPES

	ISTJ	INTJ	ISFJ	INFJ	ISTP	INTP	ISFP	INFP
Lead	IS	IN	IS	IN	IT	IT	IF	IF
Auxiliary	ET	ET	EF	EF	ES	EN	ES	EN
Tertiary	EF	EF	ET	ET	EN	ES	EN	ES
Least Used	EN	ES	EN	ES	EF	EF	ET	ET

used by different individuals with relative degrees of awareness and reliability. In other words, to get at the complete dynamic within each type, we must identify a lead attitude and function, auxiliary attitude and function, tertiary attitude and function, and least preferred (inferior) attitude and function. This ordering is an outcome of each person's habits of mind. Consequently, we are more likely to be aware and make deliberate use of our lead attitude and function, while our least used attitude and function may be rarely utilized consciously. The least used is often referred to as inferior; as the lead function is superior in consciousness, the least used is inferior to consciousness. The order of conscious access, according to type theory, is as shown in table 2.

Taken together, Jung and Myers provide a shorthand model for understanding selectivity in habits of perception and judgment. This enables the type-knowledgeable person to read a four-letter abbreviation of preferences as sorted by the MBTI instrument not just as (for example) Introversion, Sensing, Thinking, and Judging (ISTJ), but rather as a dynamic preference for a dominant process of Introverted Sensing supported by an auxiliary process of Extraverted Thinking. Later in the chapter is a description of the dominant and auxiliary functions for each of the types, but even as we proceed toward it, we remind you again: People are not types. We have a multiplicity of potential responses that show our complexity and capacity to adjust.

We are individuals with unique experiences, competencies, and a one-time special combination of genetic material. Like the Taoist philosophy asserting that there are patterns among changes, fixity among chaos, and movement within stability, psychological type proposes that it is the nature of humankind to live in a complex, handmade lacework of social and interpersonal relationships.[23] Habits of mind—psychological type—act in combination with other innate dispositions to influence how we perceive and judge these relationships. Perceptions and judgments, in turn, promote typical expressions in behavior that tend to be consistent and enduring. The structure that supports these habits and typical behaviors is psychological type.

Remember Polarities and Compensation

Two reminders: First, types exist due to the different poles of energy (Extraversion, Introversion), perception (Sensing, Intuition), and judgment (Thinking, Feeling); second, each of the functions provides avenues for dealing with life's challenges. There is a kind of mental compensation that occurs to allow us to utilize those "understudy functions," which often don't get much time on center stage but nonetheless stand at the ready for the moment when the lead becomes tired or ineffectual.

Basic Dynamic Purpose

The poles of psychological type create energy fields that serve particular psychological purposes in the same way a magnet must have both a positive and negative pole to create its energy field. Thus, polarity is the underlying structure of type. Keep in mind that an important structural aspect of this model is that the polarities create an energy exchange system such that energy spent in one area is compensated for in another. Consider an example of the Extraverted Intuitive type (ENFP or ENTP) who spends enormous energy at work creating and processing ideas and models throughout the day but who, at the end of the day, takes the long way home to provide quiet, reflective time to make decisions and bring order to the day's events. This enables her to be calm and attentive with her family. Without necessarily thinking, "I need to balance my type," but rather following her own impulses, she is attending to a primitive urge to take care of herself. See table 1 in chapter 1 to remind yourself of the frontline components of balance for each type in the balancing energy exchange system. Dire stories about those who ignore this basic internal urge for balance are all around us. Consider the constant distress of those who feel compelled to react to every situation or to run from the difficult situations they encounter daily. This kind of distress has consequences to health and long-term well-being.

Or think of the executive with preferences for Extraverted Thinking (ESTJ or ENTJ) who spends all day extraverting his Thinking judgments around a group of close associates, but who fails to allow himself time for reflection, for internal evaluation of priorities. His failure to listen to his internal voice will almost certainly lead to burnout as he depletes his natural energy without providing time for renewal by balancing his Introverted and Extraverted needs. It is easy for such individuals to feel shallow, to become rigidly judgmental, or to simply see all things as untrustworthy. It makes sense that if he distrusts his own instincts to the extent of hurting himself, how or why should he trust anyone else? This lack of balance is likely to be experienced acutely by those around him who endure the behavior born of such rigidity and narrow focus. If he only had the awareness of the effects of his behavior on others and the systems within which he operates, he might feel compelled to pay more attention to the internal voice calling for balance in his life. If this situation continues long enough, his internal exchange system will essentially force him to use a least preferred cognitive function, the one most unlike his dominant function, to direct his focus of attention and making of judgments. This usurping of power by the least used mental function will make his life, and the lives of those around him, utterly unsettled and miserable until he takes the time to attend to his need for balance. (The full nature of this process is discussed in chapter 4.)

Dynamic Compensation

In later chapters, similar analysis is provided to illustrate the rules of compensation for each variety of type dynamics. For Jung, compensation is largely an unconscious process by which individuals simply take care of themselves without much ado.[24] Nonetheless, understanding the process of compensation is essential because it provides balancing of the mental processes, adaptation to situational demands, and an understanding of the complexity of behavioral expressions that emerge for each individual.

We could say in general that an individual with preferences for INFP is an Introverted Feeling type who extraverts Intuition, and that the two attitudes work with each other to create a balance between perceiving and judging information. But in real life, due to the situation of the moment or to individual life history, the rule of compensation may work very differently and lead to very different behaviors for one INFP when compared to another. Typically calm, reserved, and gentle individuals, INFPs may nevertheless be very aggressive, energetic, and analytical when presenting their ideals.

Tension Among the Dimensions

To adapt to the world and adjust to the variety of demands facing us, we call on the dimension of ourselves that seems most appropriate at the time; in addition, an internal dynamic dance plays among these dimensions that make up personality type. Simply sorting ourselves along the type dimensions, say as an ESTJ, is a shorthand way to describe the dynamic tension going on between Extraverted Thinking and Introverted Sensing. Importantly, this dynamic between Judgment and Perception and between Introversion and Extraversion directly influences our typical expressions in everyday life.

As mentioned, many important influences on a person's behavior are outside the realm of personality type. While type can be a profound force in how we experience life, people are not types. Discussing his own descriptors of the different personality types, Jung said, "Every individual is an exception to the rule. Hence one can never give a description of a type, no matter how complete, that would apply to more than one individual, despite the fact that in some ways it aptly characterizes thousands of others. Conformity is one side of man, uniqueness is the other."[25] Understand, then, that the personality is a complex energy exchange system, which is balancing and compensating in perpetuity.

Habits Leading to Expressions

It might be satisfying if the formula for predicting behavior and for understanding others was a simple set of letters. But basic formulas serve only limited ends. Individuals are so complex that we should truly be delighted to have even a glimpse of the basic energy, perceptual, and decision-making patterns inherent in each person. Given that type expressions give you a set of clues—not the complete psychological story—you have an opportunity to begin exploring ways to further understand and value different perspectives within a rational framework.

When first learning about type, many people want a detailed and thorough description of this dynamic for each type. This is often motivated by the desire for something that will explain it all without gaps or overlaps, but by now you know this is not a constructive or even accurate use of type. Observing typical expressions of type is far more representative of the adapting, responding, and developing adult. Any detailed description would tend to ignore many other influences on each individual and imply a more fixed system of psychology than really exists. Consequently, we will examine typical expressions of type dynamics using adjectives and phrases rather than entire paragraphs or other long prose descriptors. These descriptors give a very clear image of the patterns without precluding the host of other qualities that are also likely to be present.

The descriptors in table 3 are of typical expressions of attitudes and functions such as Extraverted Thinking, Introverted Sensing, and so on. As described in the Preface, our research began by examining all of the research we could find on psychological type.[26] Each study was examined to make sure that the people in the study were typical (no clinical groups, for example) and that the behaviors under study were typical—reading habits or management practices, perhaps, but not depression or eating disorders. We sought to identify research that used adequately large samples, sufficiently controlled conditions, and included assessment of behavior via both a self-report format and observation reports from others. Once all of the studies were selected, we began looking for overlaps in the results. When the same descriptor for a type showed up in three different studies, it met our criteria for inclusion here. One reason we do not use full-paragraph type descriptions is that too often (in our experience about thirty-five percent of the time) the detailed descriptions simply do not work for individuals though they may in fact verify that the MBTI inventory sorted their preferences correctly.[27] Our goal is to present you with kernels of truth about the typical expressions of the preferences, both in terms of their natural expression and of their expression by people experiencing stress. Thus for each type you have descriptors of the normal, well-rested expressions of preferences, and descriptors of those preferences when an individual feels pushed, stressed, or particularly worn out. Keep in mind that the descriptors generally capture the dominant use of each pattern (Introverted Intuition or

Extraverted Sensing); about half to two-thirds of the patterns will still apply when the preference pattern is identified as the auxiliary or supporting attitude and function. We will first look at the descriptors of the attitudes and functions and then at how the combinations of these expressions make up the dominant and auxiliary dynamic.

More Than a Formula

Instead of seeing a person with Introverted Intuitive preferences as Mr. or Ms. Abstract, or one with Extraverted Feeling preferences as Mr. or Ms. Sweetness, recall that a typical expression merely reflects the way one *generally* responds. Type neither predicts competence in a given role nor reveals the richness of life experience brought to the task at hand. *Preference does not equal competence!* If you too quickly dismiss a person because of perceived type expressions, you have foolishly eliminated opportunities for talented individuals to contribute to your life and work. By definition, psychological type is a messy complexity that provides a mere first step toward understanding oneself and others.

Fragments of All Preferences

You can and should see some of yourself in all of the lists of type preference descriptors. As argued earlier, healthy development suggests that an individual may call upon any function in either attitude as required by a given situation. A story illustrates the difference between type preference and a situational type expression.

Roger and a friend who knows type were walking together in an unfamiliar city, trying to follow directions to a restaurant. Seeing their confused expressions, a passerby said with a smile, "You two look a bit lost. May I help you find your way somewhere?" After getting them back on course, she cheerfully went on her way. As she did so, Roger's friend said, "Thank heaven for Extraverted Feeling types!" Roger's response: "No. Thank heaven for Extraverted Feeling, regardless of who is doing it!"

The point is, neither Roger nor his friend knew that stranger's MBTI preferences, and ultimately it didn't matter. What did matter was that in a moment of seeing two lost people, she chose to use an Extraverted Feeling expression to respond to the situation.

We began this deliberation with the premise that type is about how we adapt and respond to the world given our patterns of

TABLE 3

EXPRESSIONS OF THE ATTITUDES AND FUNCTIONS

INTROVERTED INTUITION

(Dominant for INFJ, INTJ; Auxiliary for ENFJ, ENTJ)
values knowledge for its own sake
introspective
scholarly
likes ideas and theory
evaluates motives
sees to the heart of important problems
appreciative
formal
values intellectual matters

Under stress may become
withdrawn, retiring, dreamy, hardheaded, reserved

Introverted Intuition is pulled toward the future and toward possibilities. This function is like an inner eye focused on what could be, rather than what is. As a consequence, individuals with this preference often seem scholarly or studious, as if looking toward the center of a problem. This tendency may show up as, for example, a knack for summarizing a long conversation in one sentence. Interpersonally, individuals who prefer Introverted Intuition are seen by others as calm and capable of concentrated attention.

EXTRAVERTED INTUITION

(Dominant for ENTP, ENFP; Auxiliary for INTP, INFP)
action-oriented innovator
adaptable
verbally fluent
resourceful
active, enthusiastic
friendly, jolly
uninhibited
likes rapid tempo

Under stress may become
distracted, impulsive, unrealistic in expectations, hasty, noisy

Extraverted Intuition has an enormous appetite for external possibilities. This leads to quick pursuit of ideas in conversations, fast-paced search for information, and interpersonal style that seems to adapt at will. Because individuals with this preference are drawn to many different experiences, they often have a resource bank of ideas to call on to aid them in discussions. This function exerts a fun-loving attitude—an interpersonal style of active engagement in whatever is going on.

TABLE 3 (CONTINUED)

EXPRESSIONS OF THE ATTITUDES AND FUNCTIONS

INTROVERTED SENSING

(Dominant for ISFJ, ISTJ; Auxiliary for ESFJ, ESTJ)
thoughtful realist
unhurried
tests ideas with facts
careful, calm, and steady
consistent and reliable
fastidious
loyal
unassuming

Under stress may become

stingy, unemotional, overly conventional

Introverted Sensing is a function drawn to the concrete and specific details of any information presented. This leads to carefully moderated responses to questions or tasks. People with this preference believe in economy of effort, that performing a task consistently and persistently now will conserve the energy that otherwise would have to be spent later to correct mistakes. Because they are pulled to immediate concrete information, they often seem very realistic.

EXTRAVERTED SENSING

(Dominant for ESTP, ESFP; Auxiliary for ISTP, ISFP)
action-oriented realist
practical
reliable
forceful
thorough
excitable
good-natured
knows who, what, when, where
good at easing tensions

Under stress may become

unscrupulous, unkind, opportunistic, rigid

Extraverted Sensing is expressed in quick-paced reporting in factual, pragmatic terms. Often pulled toward action-oriented responses, individuals with this preference seem efficiently forceful about getting the job done. After giving thorough attention to the specifics of any given situation, such people often have a good-natured response that suggests that whatever the problem, it can be solved.

TABLE 3 (CONTINUED)

EXPRESSIONS OF THE ATTITUDES AND FUNCTIONS

INTROVERTED THINKING

(Dominant for INTP, ISTP; Auxiliary for ENTP, ESTP)

reflective reasoner
quiet, detachedly curious
analyzes vs. runs his or her world
organizes ideas
values intellectual matters
seen as independent and autonomous
often critical and skeptical
original and imaginative
often unconventional

Under stress may become

rebellious and nonconforming, restless, self-centered, and defensive

Introverted Thinking is a pattern often experienced by others as a detached curiosity. This curiosity leads those who prefer it toward active but quiet analysis of nearly everything. Reveling in the complexity required to deal with the world, they are frequently seen as independent minded (their model of how things work may be very different from mainstream thought, but INTPs have their reasons). Interpersonally, they may express skeptical acceptance of the world around them.

EXTRAVERTED THINKING

(Dominant for ESTJ, ENTJ; Auxiliary for INTJ, ISTJ)

action-oriented thinker
critical, resourceful
proactive and systematic
has a basic formula about the world
energetic, prefers a rapid pace
reasonable and analytical
expressive, fluent
mentally versatile
high aspirations

Under stress may become

arrogant and condescending, reckless and aggressive, opportunistic

Extraverted Thinking is a mental pattern of actively analyzing experience and information, and expressing this analysis in an energetic fashion. Individuals with this preference are often seen as having a plan, or model, to help adapt to and manage the world around them. Resourceful with ideas and suggestions, Extraverted Thinkers are often fluent critics and have ideas on how to improve just about anything put before them.

TABLE 3 (CONTINUED)

EXPRESSIONS OF THE ATTITUDES AND FUNCTIONS

INTROVERTED FEELING

(Dominant for ISFP, INFP; Auxiliary for ENFP, ESFP)

reflective harmonizer

quiet, deferent

cares about values and people

artistic (aesthetic)

introspective

unusual or unconventional thinking

arouses liking and acceptance in people

sensitive

Under stress may become

irritable, touchy, suspicious, or undependable

Introverted Feeling is often exhibited in quiet, deferent attitudes. Individuals expressing these preferences seem sensitive to the environment around them. Because the first response of Introverted Feeling is to accept the other person, a great deal of energy is spent helping the other to be comfortable. Given the inclination to focus on values as a basis for reacting to events, individuals with this preference seem unconventional to those with a focus on logical answers.

EXTRAVERTED FEELING

(Dominant for ESFJ, ENFJ; Auxiliary for INFJ, ISFJ)

action-oriented cooperator

sympathetic

sociable and friendly

empathetic

affiliative, warm

wants inclusion

outgoing, gregarious

idealistic

facially expressive

energetic

Under stress may become

impulsive, hasty, sentimental, fussy, self-dramatizing

Extraverted Feeling is expressed in an energetic, cooperative fashion with attention to social interaction in sympathetic and friendly behaviors. Often given to expressive engagement with others, when Extraverted Feeling is being used it appears to be drawn to others seeking inclusion in social affairs. While given to a cooperative spirit, individuals with this preference act quickly to address issues they see, believing they can achieve an idealistic goal that could help improve the human condition.

perception and judgment. As the patterns become clearer, it seems more obvious that knowing your own dynamic aids in understanding your interpersonal style, and that studying the gifts of other types uncovers your interpersonal blind spots. This self-knowledge can lead to insight regarding your relationships, leadership, learning methods, and areas of needed development.

The complexity and richness of type begins to reveal itself when you combine the expression of the preferred perception and decision-making processes. Using table 3, you can create an impressionistic portrait of a psychological type by combining the descriptors of its dominant and auxiliary functions. An even more complete impression of the type dynamic can be gained by connecting each set of descriptors for the relevant lead and auxiliary role of each type. From this you begin to see how important it is to consider type valuable as an expression of heart—the patterns of psychological comfort.

As we pull the preferences together to find an expression of the whole type, remember that only portions of the auxiliary descriptors will hold true for each type. For Introverts in general, the Extraverted auxiliary is toned down somewhat in the amount of energy exhibited, though the term may be accurate. For example, an INTP who has Extraverted Intuition as auxiliary may not be seen as generally jolly, uninhibited, or friendly; however, in a comfortable environment among friends, those terms may be quite applicable. This is the pattern for all of the Extravert descriptions when applied as the auxiliary expressions of Introverts.

Conversely, those who have an Introverted auxiliary may be initially inclined to deny that descriptions of Introversion apply to them. Yet when they think about the times they allow themselves to be reflective, quiet, and calm, they may find that Introversion does indeed describe them at such times. Whatever your type, keep in mind that we are less likely to be aware of the typical expressions of our auxiliary. But a developed, mature, appropriate expression of the auxiliary is probably clear on certain occasions.

As you read the descriptors, consider both the rewarding and the problematic interactions you've had with various individuals. You may never know the type preferences of those involved, but there is actually no need to; it is enough to know that the expressions you listen to daily are at least partially the result of orderly differences in perception and judgment. Sometimes it helps just to know that you really may be on the same wavelength with some folks but not with others, and likewise that problem areas are not necessarily the result of diabolical plots spawned in the dark of night to irritate you to distraction and stymie all your good work!

Pondering type differences may lead you to see that the various ways people express themselves has a lot to say about their habits of mind, and that how such variations are interpreted by a given observer has a lot to say about the habits of mind of that observer. For example, people who are expressive and warm about personal experiences may merely exhibit a natural expression of Extraverted Feeling. Yet some observers may suggest that such behavior is designed to manipulate or control those around them. Who is right? These communication questions are rich, and we consider them in depth in chapter 6, but to gain the most from that discussion you need to understand the patterns of expression laid out in table 4. Knowing that there are tangible, legitimate differences in perception and judgment opens the doors of communication and provides the foundation for valuing differences.

As we have explored, type is an elegant model of habits of mind—the ways we seek energy, attend to information, and make decisions. It features a system of ordering the habits that is most useful and pragmatic, and demonstrates that people seem to have primary and secondary styles that are most evident in their typical expressions and ways of doing things.

Through the complexity and sufficiency of the model of psychological type, we have the opportunity to make better judgments about our interactions, more choices in what to say and do to be influential, and a better understanding of our personal history. But as is true of any model, no matter how constructive and incisive, it can be distorted and misused. Those seeking shortcuts in understanding and in making sense of situations will no doubt use this model as a sword to direct and control others. In the chapters ahead we will continue to explore the natural expressions of the preferences, the importance of the inferior or least used function, the moral issues with using psychological type, and how these types fit into communication and valuing.

Through each page we should keep in the forefront of our minds that the goal is to extend human understanding and development. Any other use works against the intent of the theory. The simple fact is that millions who have taken the *Myers-Briggs Type Indicator* personality inventory have merely scratched the surface of what type can provide in their lives. With studious attention to the ideas in this and the next several chapters, we can move closer to the realization of those for whom type means so very much: pathways of valuing and development that raise the quality of our psychological lives.

TABLE 4

DESCRIPTORS FOR THE SIXTEEN TYPES

EXTRAVERTED SENSING TYPES

TYPE	
DOMINANT/LEAD FUNCTION DESCRIPTORS *Most aware of . . .*	**AUXILIARY/SUPPORTER FUNCTION DESCRIPTORS** *Fully functioning but less aware of . . .*

ESTP

Extraverted Sensing	**Introverted Thinking**
realistic, action-oriented	reflective reasoner
practical	quiet, detachedly curious
reliable, thorough	analyzes vs. runs his or her world
forceful	seen as independent
excitable	and autonomous
good-natured	often critical and skeptical
knows who, what, when, where	often unconventional
good at easing tensions	original and imaginative

Under stress may become

unkind, unscrupulous, opportunistic, rigid	*rebellious, nonconforming, restless, defensive*

ESFP

Extraverted Sensing	**Introverted Feeling**
realistic, action-oriented	reflective harmonizer
practical	quiet, deferent
reliable, thorough	cares for values and people
forceful	artistic
excitable	introspective
good-natured	unusual or unconventional thinking
knows who, what, when, where	arouses liking and acceptance in people
good at easing tensions	sensitive

Under stress may become

unkind, unscrupulous, opportunistic, rigid	*irritable, touchy, suspicious, or undependable*

TABLE 4 (CONTINUED)

DESCRIPTORS FOR THE SIXTEEN TYPES

EXTRAVERTED INTUITIVE TYPES

TYPE	
DOMINANT/LEAD FUNCTION DESCRIPTORS *Most aware of . . .*	**AUXILIARY/SUPPORTER FUNCTION DESCRIPTORS** *Fully functioning but less aware of . . .*

ENFP

Extraverted Intuition	**Introverted Feeling**
action-oriented innovator	reflective harmonizer
adaptable	quiet, deferent
verbally fluent	cares for values and people
resourceful	artistic
active	introspective
likes rapid tempo	unusual or unconventional
enthusiastic	thinking
friendly, jolly	arouses liking and acceptance
uninhibited	in people
	sensitive

Under stress may become

distracted, impulsive, unrealistic in expectations, hasty, noisy	*irritable, touchy, suspicious, or undependable*

ENTP

Extraverted Intuition	**Introverted Thinking**
action-oriented innovator	reflective reasoner
adaptable	quiet, detachedly curious
verbally fluent	analyzes vs. runs his or her world
resourceful	seen as independent and
active	autonomous
likes rapid tempo	often critical and skeptical
enthusiastic	often unconventional
friendly, jolly	original and imaginative
uninhibited	

Under stress may become

distracted, impulsive, unrealistic in expectations, hasty, noisy	*rebellious, nonconforming, restless, defensive*

TABLE 4 (CONTINUED)

DESCRIPTORS FOR THE SIXTEEN TYPES

EXTRAVERTED THINKING TYPES

TYPE

DOMINANT/LEAD FUNCTION DESCRIPTORS	AUXILIARY/SUPPORTER FUNCTION DESCRIPTORS
Most aware of . . .	*Fully functioning but less aware of . . .*

ESTJ

Extraverted Thinking	**Introverted Sensing**
action-oriented thinker	thoughtful realist
resourceful, critical	unhurried, careful
proactive and systematic	tests ideas with facts
has a basic formula about	calm
the world	steady
energetic, likes a rapid pace	consistent and reliable
reasonable and analytical	loyal
expressive, fluent	fastidious
mentally versatile	unassuming
high aspirations	

Under stress may become

arrogant and condescending, reckless and aggressive, opportunistic	*stingy, unemotional, and overly conventional*

ENTJ

Extraverted Thinking	**Introverted Intuition**
action-oriented thinker	values knowledge for its
resourceful, critical	own sake
proactive and systematic	introspective, scholarly
has a basic formula about	likes ideas and theories
the world	evaluates motives
energetic, likes a rapid pace	sees to the heart of
reasonable and analytical	important problems
expressive, fluent	appreciative, formal
mentally versatile	values intellectual matters
high aspirations	

Under stress may become

arrogant and condescending, reckless and aggressive, opportunistic	*retiring, dreamy, hardheaded, reserved*

TABLE 4 (CONTINUED)

DESCRIPTORS FOR THE SIXTEEN TYPES

EXTRAVERTED FEELING TYPES

TYPE

DOMINANT/LEAD FUNCTION DESCRIPTORS	AUXILIARY/SUPPORTER FUNCTION DESCRIPTORS
Most aware of...	*Fully functioning but less aware of...*

ESFJ

Extraverted Feeling	**Introverted Sensing**
action-oriented	thoughtful realist
prefers cooperation	unhurried
sympathetic	tests ideas with facts
sociable and friendly	careful
affiliative	calm
warm	steady
wants inclusion	consistent and reliable
outgoing	loyal
gregarious	fastidious
idealistic	unassuming

Under stress may become

impulsive, hasty, sentimental, fussy, self-dramatizing	*stingy, unemotional, and overly conventional*

ENFJ

Extraverted Feeling	**Introverted Intuition**
action-oriented	values knowledge for its
prefers cooperation	own sake
sympathetic	introspective
sociable and friendly	scholarly
affiliative	likes ideas and theories
warm	evaluates motives
wants inclusion	sees to the heart of
outgoing	important problems
gregarious	appreciative, formal
idealistic	values intellectual matters

Under stress may become

impulsive, hasty, sentimental, fussy, self-dramatizing	*retiring, dreamy, hardheaded, reserved*

TABLE 4 (CONTINUED)

DESCRIPTORS FOR THE SIXTEEN TYPES

INTROVERTED SENSING TYPES

TYPE

DOMINANT/LEAD FUNCTION DESCRIPTORS	AUXILIARY/SUPPORTER FUNCTION DESCRIPTORS
Most aware of . . .	*Fully functioning but less aware of . . .*

ISTJ

Introverted Sensing	Extraverted Thinking
thoughtful realist	action-oriented thinker
unhurried	resourceful
tests ideas with facts	proactive and systematic
careful	critical
calm	has a basic formula about
steady	the world
consistent and reliable	energetic, likes a rapid pace
loyal	reasonable and analytical
fastidious	expressive, fluent
unassuming	mentally versatile
	high aspirations

Under stress may become

stingy, unemotional, and overly conventional	*arrogant and condescending, reckless and aggressive, opportunistic*

ISFJ

Introverted Sensing	Extraverted Feeling
thoughtful realist	action-oriented
unhurried	prefers cooperation
tests ideas with facts	sympathetic
careful	sociable and friendly
calm	affiliative, warm
steady	wants inclusion
consistent and reliable	outgoing, gregarious
loyal	idealistic
fastidious	
unassuming	

Under stress may become

stingy, unemotional, and overly conventional	*impulsive, hasty, sentimental, fussy, self-dramatizing*

TABLE 4 (CONTINUED)

DESCRIPTORS FOR THE SIXTEEN TYPES

INTROVERTED INTUITIVE TYPES

TYPE	
DOMINANT/LEAD FUNCTION DESCRIPTORS	**AUXILIARY/SUPPORTER FUNCTION DESCRIPTORS**
Most aware of...	*Fully functioning but less aware of...*

INTJ

Introverted Intuition	**Extraverted Thinking**
values knowledge for its own sake	action-oriented thinker
introspective	resourceful
scholarly	proactive and systematic
likes ideas and theories	critical
evaluates motives	has a basic formula about the world
sees to the heart of important problems	energetic, likes a rapid pace
appreciative, formal	reasonable and analytical
values intellectual matters	expressive, fluent
	mentally versatile
	high aspirations

Under stress may become

retiring, dreamy, hardheaded, reserved	*arrogant and condescending, reckless and aggressive, opportunistic*

INFJ

Introverted Intuition	**Extraverted Feeling**
values knowledge for its own sake	action-oriented
introspective	prefers cooperation
scholarly	sympathetic
likes ideas and theories	sociable and friendly
evaluates motives	affiliative, warm
sees to the heart of important problems	wants inclusion
appreciative, formal	outgoing, gregarious
values intellectual matters	idealistic

Under stress may become

retiring, dreamy hardheaded, reserved	*impulsive, hasty, sentimental, fussy, self-dramatizing*

TABLE 4 (CONTINUED)

DESCRIPTORS FOR THE SIXTEEN TYPES

INTROVERTED THINKING TYPES

TYPE	
DOMINANT/LEAD FUNCTION DESCRIPTORS	**AUXILIARY/SUPPORTER FUNCTION DESCRIPTORS**
Most aware of . . .	*Fully functioning but less aware of . . .*

ISTP

Introverted Thinking	**Extraverted Sensing**
reflective reasoner	realistic, action-oriented
quiet, detachedly curious	practical
analyzes vs. runs his or her world	reliable, thorough
seen as independent	forceful
and autonomous	excitable
often critical and skeptical	good-natured
often unconventional	knows who, what, when, where
original and imaginative	good at easing tensions

Under stress may become

rebellious, nonconforming, restless, defensive	*unkind, unscrupulous, opportunistic, rigid*

INTP

Introverted Thinking	**Extraverted Intuition**
reflective reasoner	action-oriented innovator
quiet, detachedly curious	adaptable
analyzes vs. runs his or her world	verbally fluent
seen as independent	resourceful
and autonomous	active
often critical and skeptical	likes rapid tempo
often unconventional	enthusiastic
original and imaginative	friendly, jolly
	uninhibited

Under stress may become

rebellious, nonconforming, restless, defensive	*distracted, impulsive, hasty, noisy, unrealistic in expectations*

TABLE 4 (CONTINUED)

DESCRIPTORS FOR THE SIXTEEN TYPES

INTROVERTED FEELING TYPES

TYPE	
DOMINANT/LEAD FUNCTION DESCRIPTORS *Most aware of . . .*	**AUXILIARY/SUPPORTER FUNCTION DESCRIPTORS** *Fully functioning but less aware of . . .*

ISFP

Introverted Feeling	**Extraverted Sensing**
reflective harmonizer	realistic, action-oriented
quiet, deferent	practical
cares for values and people	reliable, thorough
artistic	forceful
introspective	excitable
unusual or unconventional thinking	good-natured
arouses liking and acceptance in people	knows who, what, when, where
sensitive	good at easing tensions

Under stress may become

irritable, touchy, suspicious, or undependable	*unkind, unscrupulous, opportunistic, rigid*

INFP

Introverted Feeling	**Extraverted Intuition**
reflective harmonizer	action-oriented innovator
quiet, deferent	adaptable
cares for values and people	verbally fluent
artistic	resourceful
introspective	active
unusual or unconventional thinking	likes rapid tempo
arouses liking and acceptance in people	enthusiastic
sensitive	friendly, jolly
	uninhibited

Under stress may become

irritable, touchy, suspicious, or undependable	*distracted, impulsive, hasty, noisy, unrealistic in expectations*

ELEMENTS OF BALANCE

Processes That Keep Us Mindful

sychological type is about balancing acts. Within the context of human mental health, balancing is a process, not a state of being. If we accept Jung and Myers' definition of type, then it is clear that the balancing of a person's extraverted and introverted energy through the perceiving and judging functions is essential to healthy adaptation and responsiveness. Balancing is an ongoing requirement for a person's continued development and growth. For example, the individual who gets stuck in judgment becomes judgmental and rigid. Without attention to perception, this individual is out of balance and will begin to become stale, one-sided, and uncomfortable. Likewise, the person stuck in perception becomes incapable of making decisions, which leads to an equally stale and uncomfortable personality. Imagine the psyche as a heavy-duty kitchen sponge, with ideas and data perceptions providing the liquid necessary for it to work and decision-making criteria providing its fiber. For the sponge to work best, liquid and fiber must balance properly. If the sponge is too dry, lacking all liquid, it becomes brittle and will crumble in your hands if you use it for serious work. In the same manner, if the sponge is supersaturated with water—like the psyche overindulged in perception—it merely flops over the edges of your hand and is too soft and porous to be used for serious work. When we think of psychological balance in this way, we can see that type gives us a different way to understand our psychological discomforts—they may be a sign that our adaptation to experience has slowed and we are out of balance. The message from the psyche is: "Attend to your own processes."

As discussed earlier, type dynamics are expressed and identified as the combination of attitudes (Extraversion and Introversion) with the mental functions of Sensing, Intuition, Thinking, and

Feeling. We can identify the Extraverted–Introverted function dynamic for each type by sorting the preferences for the Judgment and Perception orientations as shown in table 1. The power and richness of the dynamic process driving our Extraverted and Introverted mental functions were fully explored in the last chapter, but a brief summary is appropriate here before moving to the next level.

Type theory suggests that all mental functions are used in varying degrees and that the complete dynamic within each type consists of a lead (dominant) attitude and function, a secondary (auxiliary) attitude and function, a third (tertiary) attitude and function, and a least-preferred (inferior) attitude and function. The order of these preferences in an individual is an outcome of the habits of mind enjoyed by that person. Consequently, we are more likely to be aware of, and make deliberate use of, our dominant function, while our least used attitude and function may be rarely utilized consciously. This is why the least used function is referred to as inferior; the lead function is superior because we are more conscious of it, and the least used is called inferior not because it is less worthy or less important but because we are least conscious of it. For a full table of the hierarchy of functions for each type and discussions about type dynamics, you may refer to chapter 2. Chapter 4 will look at the richness and lessons of the inferior function in great detail. We have taken time to review the concept of type dynamics here because it is central to understanding the nature of each typology. As noted, these attitudes and functions perform a variety of balancing acts that enable each of us to experience life fully and respond to life with purpose. But there is more.

In addition to evidence for type dynamics, there are data to support expressions of various interactions of the type preferences. For example, an ENTP has the dynamic of Extraverted Intuition with Introverted Thinking. This type also has distinct behavioral expressions that result from interactions between Extraversion and Perception (EP), which we will refer to as the *outer image;* between the perceiving function and Perceiving orientation (NP), which we call the *motivator;* between the judgment function and Perceiving orientation (TP), which we call *inner tension;* and between the perceiving and judging functions (NT), which we call the *cognitive core.* Each of these interactions has a unique set of expressions that truly show the beauty and complexity of each type.

In our research, we sought evidence for the interactions in the same way we identified evidence for the various expressions of

TABLE 5

ELEMENTS OF BALANCE FOR EACH TYPE

	EXTRAVERTED TYPES							
	ESTJ	ENTJ	ESFJ	ENFJ	ESTP	ENTP	ESFP	ENFP
Outer Image	EJ	EJ	EJ	EJ	EP	EP	EP	EP
Motivator	TJ	TJ	FJ	FJ	SP	NP	SP	NP
Inner Tension	SJ	NJ	SJ	NJ	TP	TP	FP	FP
Cognitive Core	ST	NT	SF	NF	ST	NT	SF	NF

	INTROVERTED TYPES							
	ISTJ	INTJ	ISFJ	INFJ	ISTP	INTP	ISFP	INFP
Outer Image	IJ	IJ	IJ	IJ	IP	IP	IP	IP
Motivator	TJ	TJ	FJ	FJ	SP	NP	SP	NP
Inner Tension	SJ	NJ	SJ	NJ	TP	TP	FP	FP
Cognitive Core	ST	NT	SF	NF	ST	NT	SF	NF

preferences. To meet our criteria for inclusion, evidence had to come from at least three different and sound research sources and had to be verified by our database. The terms *outer image, motivator, inner tension,* and *cognitive core* are based on the central psychological issue in each kind of interaction.

For each of the types, the interactions among the preferences are as shown in table 5.

Outer Image

How you are perceived by another person during a quick first meeting might surprise you, but the type interaction we call outer image is like a mirror that shows the often distorted impressions others receive. Since abundant evidence suggests that judgments are made about you within the first fifteen seconds of an interaction, the importance of gaining this self-awareness cannot be overstated. It helps us understand how so many quick misjudgments are made and how we might ask more appropriate questions of each other in order to get past the outer image.

Understanding outer image provides the motivation to pause before we jump to conclusions about people when we first meet them—perhaps we'll better understand why they may behave so differently during an introductory conversation than in more in-depth interactions. It also shows how we ourselves can be so easily misread by others upon first meeting. For example, an energetic and spontaneous EP may completely misread a reserved and rest-less IP as being disinterested. At a minimum, we are invited to con-sider how we present ourselves and to suspend judgment on inter-actional styles different from our own.

To the question, "If someone took an interpersonal snapshot of you during the early moments of conversation, how might they describe you in the interaction?" we get a match between the answer to the question and the descriptors of the interactions of the attitudes and orientations (EJ, EP, IJ, IP). Those descriptors and answers interact to the descriptors shown in table 6.

Consider these snapshots of outer image the next time you meet an acquaintance or someone new to you. What are you responding to in them, and what may they be responding to in you? We have seen this information have transformative effects in inter-view skills training and executive coaching. As the saying goes, you never get a second chance to make a first impression. Understanding these interactions and making considered choices in your future behavior helps you make the most of new opportunities.

Symbolic Elements of Balance

After analysis of all the MBTI research, we searched for patterns in the data. If, as Jung suggested, psychological type is a kind of com-pass that guides a person's behavior, then it follows that the indi-vidual is the centerpoint of type. If, as he further speculated, we carry within us the history of patterns of human thought in the form of archetypes, then type itself is a later development of an archetypal system in the evolution of human consciousness.[28] With these possibilities before us, exploring the interactions and their symbols is a worthy pursuit indeed.

Motivators

Unfortunately, many talented and capable individuals miss oppor-tunities because they are unaware of how their outer images are perceived by others. Likewise, many people feel unmotivated and are not sure how to put life into tasks or work. This results in unhappy experiences and poor evaluations.

TABLE 6

OUTER IMAGE

ADAPTABLE LOOKING

EP
Extraversion and Perception
active and energetic
seeks novel experiences
informal and spontaneous
often uninhibited, likes rapid tempo

IP
Introversion and Perception
adventurous but reserved
changeable, nonconforming
restless and individualistic
tends to delay action

DECISIVE LOOKING

EJ
Extraversion and Judgment
fast moving and energetic
confident looking and charming
often conforms
talkative, sometimes blustery
conscientious

IJ
Introversion and Judgment
introspective and persevering
often quiet and modest
deferent but hard to convince
may overcontrol impulses

Viewing this issue through the lens of type, an important insight leaps out. Regardless of preference for Introversion or Extraversion, a special motivation for engaging with the world is set in motion when the external orientation (J or P) interacts with its matching Extraverted function; consequently, all energy is directed externally and with the same purpose. When the Perceiving orientation interacts with either Sensing or Intuition (whichever is the preferred perceiving mode), or when the Judging orientation inter-

TABLE 7

MOTIVATORS

SP

Sensing With Perception
adaptable realist
focused on the present
seeks new, present experiences
adapts to immediate situation
efficient with personal energy
keen awareness of the present
believer in economy of effort

If natural motivators are denied may become
distracted, inattentive, unstable, lazy

NP

Intuition With Perception
adaptable innovator
independent
seeks out new challenges
unconventional
challenging
fluent and expressive
nonconforming
imaginative
original

If natural motivators are denied may become
fickle, pleasure seeking, distractible, unable to delay gratification, restless

acts with either Thinking or Feeling (whichever is the preferred judgment mode) there is an inspired cooperation between the two, as if each is egging the other on to heights unattainable by either one alone. So, the motivating interactions are SP, NP, TJ, and FJ.

For SP and NP the motivation/exhilaration may be experienced as a sense of limitlessness, flow, and lack of boundaries, like a fully rigged ship on a smooth, wide ocean under a clear sky with perfect winds at your back. For FJ and TJ the exhilaration may be experienced as a keen sense of steady accomplishment with clearly defined needs, parameters, and priorities. Their ship has navi-

TABLE 7 (CONTINUED)

MOTIVATORS

FJ
▪

Feeling With Judgment
benevolent administrator
responsive
observant of people and their needs
informal
expressive and energized in relationships

If natural motivators are denied may become
overly evaluative of others' motivations, preoccupied

TJ
▪

Thinking With Judgment

logical decision maker
tough-minded
analytical
executive
critical, often skeptical
precise
deliberate
steady
ambitious

If natural motivators are denied may become
tense, stern, hardheaded, dominant, conceited

gated the ocean, has land in sight, and is using the wind to execute the perfect docking.

When people were given the instructions, "List the adjectives that describe what your experiences are when the moment is 'just right'; what are you typically engaged in doing, or not doing, when this feeling is triggered?" the ensuing descriptors (shown in table 7) match those of the interactions of orientations and the associated function (SP, NP, TJ, FJ). In addition, when asked to consider what might become of this motivated spirit if it is denied, there is a list of "may becomes." When these natural motivators are kept at bay for any great length of time those behaviors may emerge.

Learning about our natural motivators provides us with a key to affirm our experiences. It also provides the road map for exploring both more opportunities that allow for this interaction as well as the potential consequences of living and working in a situation that continually denies these very natural urges and needs. The suggestion is not that we must have working environments that always allow these preferences to be expressed, but that we plan activities that encourage their regular expression. For example, if present-focused seekers of new experiences like those with SP preferences live all day in the critical, analytical, tough-minded environment preferred by TJs without providing themselves with outlets for their fluid adaptability, then two outcomes are probable. First, they are likely to become distracted or lazy and consequently reduce their contributions at work. Second, the TJs are likely to believe the SPs are resistant and difficult.

If you supervise or manage others at work or at home, do you have a sufficient understanding of the various motivators that provide the basic personal satisfaction needed for them to do a good job? Are you in an environment that provides opportunities for your natural motivators to express themselves? As you plan activities and experiences for family members, you might keep this in mind when assessing whether the program in question will affirm the natural motivators at work in their types. What may seem to an NP parent like an idyllic camp or school environment could actually bring out the worst in the FJ youngster who is forced to attend. Type should never be the only data point used in making these determinations, but taking it into consideration can contribute greatly to illuminating our blind spots.

Inner Tension

Just as we need time for our natural motivating force to express itself outwardly, we need space to allow our private, internal world an opportunity to flourish. Beyond our Introverted mental function, we need to recognize and honor the internal push and pull we experience occasionally as part of our typology. This process, like that of our outer presentation and our natural motivators, is essential to a healthy recognition that our orientation to the world calls on one aspect of us while our inner operations call on another aspect of our experience. We each have a built-in mechanism that serves as an action inhibitor, for it calls on us to look inward.

Regardless of a preference for Introversion or Extraversion, this mechanism operates as the interaction between our preferred orientation (J or P) and our Introverted mental function. These interactions (SJ, NJ, TP, and FP) are experienced as a tension between outer orientation and inner mental work. For example, in the SJ interaction the orientation for Judging pulls toward decision making and closure even as the Introverted Sensing function wants to gather more data. In the TP interaction, the orientation for Perceiving creates a strong pull to remain open and to gather more information even as Introverted Thinking urges making a competent, analytical decision.

Asked to think back on a poor decision and to answer the questions, "What are you like when you realize you have either decided too quickly or waited too long for a decision? How might the people in your life experience you while you are in the midst of that process?" the descriptors intersect with those of the type interactions noted in table 8. Asked how they might be viewed by others if they stay in this psychological state too long, a further list of verified "may becomes" was generated.

Note that this does not describe those times of agitation when everything is wrong and everyone around you knows it. Rather, this interaction looks fairly calm externally, but feels uncomfortable inside. We can think of it as the internal frustration that often precedes a breakthrough of some kind. This interaction is perhaps the most difficult to understand precisely because we are so internally focused that we are unaware of how we appear to the rest of the world. All types feel internal unease; their resulting behavior often is an adaptive, socially acceptable response to the condition. Table 8 delineates how others see us behaving while that is going on.

These interactions present us with information about the times we merely go through the motions in outer life because we are actually focused on processing information in our inner life. As noted, this is at odds with the external pulls indicated by our typological orientation. When we begin to feel an internal fire, a rush to get on with it or the laboring sense that we would get on with it if we had enough information, then our system of dealing with the world is bordering on imbalance.

Two quick examples illustrate the significance of this interaction. After exclaiming that SJs "don't make bad decisions," a number of ESTJ/ESFJ women in separate workshops reported to us that they knew their first marriages were ill-fated before they ever walked down the aisle. But the gifts had been given, their parents were committed to the marriage, and all of the guests were planned for. The external world confirmed the decision to get married while data in the internal world profoundly argued against it. According to their reports, all of the energy invested in the ceremony out-

TABLE 8

INNER TENSIONS

NJ

Intuition With Judgment
visionary decision maker
persistent
strives toward inner vision
driving
determined
sensitive about demands
often seen as thorough and industrious

If stuck in this "psychological place" may become
hardheaded, fussy, blustery

SJ

Sensing With Judgment
realistic decision maker
steady
reliable
seeks order in the environment
dislikes ambiguity
stable
conforming
fastidious
often moralistic
favors conservative values
does the "correct thing"

If stuck in this "psychological place" may become
overcontrolled, opportunistic, intolerant, unable to recognize their own anxiety

weighed their internal energy that was trying to alert them to problems elsewhere. Many of the SJs argued that they don't make bad
decisions, but acknowledged that some of their decisions are made
based on poor information. After confiding about their bad marital
experiences, these same women said they had never revealed them
before out of fear that others would see them as crazy.

In another example, an INFP visiting a large city 1,200 miles
from home decided to visit a special store to purchase gifts for his

TABLE 8 (CONTINUED)

INNER TENSIONS

TP

Thinking With Perception
analytical and skeptical
associates ideas in unusual ways
tolerant
often seen as clever
enjoys orderly frameworks
enjoys the environment
observant and curious

If stuck in this "psychological place" may become

hasty, evasive, self-indulgent

FP

Feeling With Perception
affiliative and adaptable
tolerant
relatively uncontrolled expression
responsive and softhearted
enjoys humor

If stuck in this "psychological place" may become

impulsive, distractible, hasty

---

two children. The store sold only stuffed animals—thousands of them. Every day for four days he went to the store on lunch breaks and after dinner and reviewed all of the choices. A friend who accompanied him observed that he was methodical, calm, and focused on making the decision, and spent an enormous amount of time looking for the right animals, the ones that felt right for his kids. Inside, however, he was anything but calm, methodical, and focused—more like confused, distracted, and irritated at himself. He simply could not decide. The reason was that his Perceptive mode took in all the information and the judgment function evaluated all the options, which leads to indecision. Like the ESTJ/ESFJ women, the INFP felt crazy—they were simple child's gifts, after all!

It is a relief to realize that the spots we get into can be explained by a rational model. Importantly, this mechanism is an alarm that encourages us to stop and ask, "What do I need in order to respond to the situation before me?" Knowing enough to ask and answer this simple question can lead to new arenas of personal growth.

Cognitive Core

Human growth depends on our ability to stretch our ways of processing and responding to information. If we fail to acknowledge tension, we are likely to pay a price by way of difficult relationships and episodes of ill health. Type gives us a way to access some of the potential stretch areas by recognizing the dynamics and interactions of our preferred functions.

At the core of this typology is the basic interaction of the preferred perceiving and judging functions (ST, SF, NT, NF). When all of the other expressions of the preferences fade, the habits of mind that result from the interactions of the mental functions provide a bedrock on which you can build an understanding of each type's world view.

To the questions "When you plan or anticipate your day, what are people likely to see or hear from you? What are you using to help you decide on the activities of the day?" the answers overlap with the descriptors of the interactions of the cognitive functions found in table 9. These are the basic descriptors that capture the most typical qualities of the types. If you were asked to identify descriptors of how you might be seen if your plans for living out each day get frequently interrupted, a variety of "may becomes" like those found in table 9 may emerge.

Clearly, there is value in recognizing one's core processes—those that feed and nourish us throughout the day. We encourage you to make sure there is time in your day to allow for your preferred way of making choices and acting. Though it is not always possible to engage in our most natural behavior, we can recognize the need to do so and be more deliberate about creating such psychological spaces.

Each aspect of the typology of individuals provides information about basic needs, drives, and requirements for balance in everyday life. Keeping an awareness of one's own processes is hard work which demands the fullest attention and recognition of one's type. The evidence suggests that type is a fact. The only question is whether we will ignore it or use it to enrich our possibilities. Type

TABLE 9

COGNITIVE CORE

ST

Sensing With Thinking
tough-minded
reasonable
matter-of-fact
practical
verifies facts—weighs, measures
orderly
self-controlled
power oriented
self-satisfied
internally consistent

If often kept from the preferred plan may become

overcontrolled, rigid, intolerant, overly conventional,
delay gratification unnecessarily

NT

Intuition With Thinking
psychologically minded
ingenious
analytical
focuses on theoretical relationships
likes autonomy
often clever
has defined interests
pride of objectivity
methodically attentive to theory, model

If often kept from the preferred plan may become

argumentative, overconfident, indifferent or wary, condescending

provides a place to begin understanding oneself and others in the context of normal human development. It takes extraordinary courage to own one's habits of mind and to recognize their limitations. It takes tremendous energy to seek to stretch beyond these habits and tendencies in order to fulfill your potential. But such courage and energy are the stuff of moral character, available to all but accessed by few.

TABLE 9 (CONTINUED)

COGNITIVE CORE

SF

Sensing With Feeling
factually oriented
gentle and modest
seeks to meet needs
expresses personal warmth
seen as compassionate
responsible
conscientious
patient with detail
focuses on things concretely affecting others

If often kept from the preferred plan may become

overly conventional, formal, despondent, or have extremely narrow interests

NF

Intuition With Feeling
tender minded
enthusiastic
insightful
seeks new projects, complexity
flexible
identifies symbolic and theoretical relationships
aesthetic
inventive, nonconforming
unconventional thought processes

If often kept from the preferred plan may become

snobbish, self-pitying, withdrawn, fearful, anxious, dreamy, distractible

4

THE TEACHER WITHIN

Lessons We Cannot Ignore

*T*eachers attempt to show us how to pay attention to information, to direct our focus on priorities. They also may reveal our ignorance. Some of our earliest experiences are with school teachers and with our parents, teachers of another kind. But as we grow older and become more judicious about how we spend our time, we make our own decisions about what is worth knowing. We become more aware of the inner voices of experience that guide us. And as we grow in maturity and understanding, we realize that the greatest teacher is the one within.

Psychological type provides a letter of introduction to one such teacher within us. Many people familiar with type refer to this teacher as the inferior function, or the least used function.[29] As the name suggests, this function is seldom called upon and used in daily life, at least not consciously; but it is not weak, unimportant, or even lacking in activity. We propose that it is best to think of the inferior function as emerging in three roles: conscious use, adaptive use, and compensatory use. (Check table 2 in chapter 2 or table 10 in this chapter for a refresher on identifying the inferior function for each type.)

Conscious Use

Conscious use of the inferior function means you intentionally call upon it to enable you to manage a situation that is somewhat out of the ordinary. Type theory suggests that someone with preferences for INFP may prefer to plan a presentation by listing as many ideas as are relevant to the topic with a focus on the value-laden content. When, for any number of reasons, that person intentionally plans a logical, orderly, systematic presentation, he or she is calling upon Extraverted Thinking to help. When used this way, the teacher within is giving two lessons: first, we can accomplish many things when we put our minds to it, and second, we have developmental needs.

Adaptive Use

Adaptive use of the inferior function is best explained by remembering times when you dealt with a situation productively but were aware that you behaved very differently than usual. You might have thought, "Gosh, I didn't know I had it in me," but the lesson here is that you do. You have the resources necessary to manage challenges as they emerge. It's a matter of adapting to the situation by using your least developed function. In this role, the teacher is quietly ensuring our success and preparing us for lessons as we reflect on our accomplishments.

Compensatory Use

Compensatory use of the least used function occurs when we are tired, highly stressed, and have depleted the natural resources found in the dominant and auxiliary functions. Some people working with psychological type refer to this as being "in the grip of your inferior function." Essentially, in lieu of a strong dominant function, the inferior seems to rise up from the unconscious and rule our behavior—sometimes for an hour, sometimes for months. The inferior function is attempting to compensate for the loss of balance within the psychological makeup of the person. Of all the taskmasters we must face, this is perhaps the sternest. It demands that we recognize the unhealthy imbalance in our life. Table 10 shows each type and its teacher or inferior function.

Lessons Too Good To Ignore

There is very little empirical data about the teacher. We have many case examples, as do others, but it is inappropriate to generalize too far from such reports. Yet the power of the teacher within us gives a compelling call to attend to many questions.

Often the conscious and adaptive use of the inferior function happens so quickly that we hardly notice it. The conscious choice of using one's inferior function may happen as a strategy for managing a particular human interaction. The adaptive use of the inferior

TABLE 10

IDENTIFYING THE INFERIOR FUNCTION

INFERIOR FOR EXTRAVERTED TYPES

	ESTJ/ENTJ	ESFJ/ENFJ	ESTP/ESFP	ENTP/ENFP
Teacher	IF	IT	IN	IS

INFERIOR FOR INTROVERTED TYPES

	ISTJ/ISFJ	INTJ/INFJ	ISTP/INTP	ISFP/INFP
Teacher	EN	ES	EF	ET

function may simply emerge as a result of the situational pressures at work on an individual. Table 11 summarizes the characteristic expressions of the teacher in conscious and adaptive ways. (Compensatory expressions are wholly different and are discussed later.)

Finally, in the compensatory use of the teacher, we have surrendered typical control to this function.[30] Because its emergence during this state often presents a raw and even distressing picture, it may have more of a psychological punch to it. In the vernacular, it is heavy artillery. The inferior function is an exacting taskmaster, but learning to use it is a necessity in the balancing of the psyche.

Our experience indicates that if one should ignore the lessons of the inferior at any point in life, the teacher's lessons will come back stronger, more demanding, and more difficult to manage. Using the inferior function simply means that your most challenging teacher has arrived and is knocking at the door. The compensatory teacher is one over whom we have the least conscious control!

The Inferior Merely Lags in Development, Not in Strength

Of the inferior function, Jung wrote that "it lags behind in the process of differentiation . . . its true significance remains unrecognized."[31] Jung points out that the inferior is "merely backward" when compared to the favored function. Keep in mind, however, that it still serves an important role in Jung's "self-balancing psyche." For example, if you become overly dependent on the expressions of your dominant function, the compensatory inferior will erupt from the unconscious to impose balance.

TABLE 11

CONSCIOUS AND ADAPTIVE USES OF THE INFERIOR

Type	Teacher	Conscious Use	Adaptive Use
ESTJ, ENTJ	IF	Choosing to be warm, friendly	Internal awareness of personal values
ESFJ, ENFJ	IT	Planning a logical presentation	Solving a human puzzle through principles
ESTP, ESFP	IN	Internal focus on future	Following a hunch
ENTP, ENFP	IS	Concentration on task details	Managing by sequencing information
ISTJ, ISFJ	EN	Expressing ideas about the future and about meaning	Changing course midstream
INTJ, INFJ	ES	Explaining current awareness	Spontaneously focusing on Sensing information
INTP, ISTP	EF	Active expressions of appreciation	Responding empathetically
ISFP, INFP	ET	Fluent verbal critique	Expressing logical connections, systems

Identifying Expressions of the Compensatory Inferior

Knowing the characteristics of the inferior of a type is not sufficient for understanding the role of the inferior in development. You must identify the expression of the inferior in your life, both the effort to consciously use it and the times when it expressed itself outside of your control. Once you feel you have identified the way this teacher operates within you, seek out information from others who have seen your inferior function in action and have them identify its effects on you and others. It is important to recognize the unique influence of the inferior from the other functions.

While you are getting a handle on the nature of the inferior function in your own life and behaviors, it is also important to realize that just identifying is not enough. The next step is to develop a method of transforming the energy and insights you gain into useful conscious material. This transformation of energy from recognition to constructive use requires hard work. Journals are very useful; having an effective personal guide works, too. Keep in mind, however, that we may not be able to directly access our fourth mental function; in some of us it is far from awareness and simply cannot be easily activated.

Reincorporating the compensatory inferior function—integrating it—means acknowledging that it has a legitimate voice in your life and can be a valuable guide when needed. Many of the lessons of the inferior function lie beyond recognition and transformation of its presence and nature. After much conscious work, you may not realize a lesson has been learned until well after the fact. It is helpful to know that your inferior function may encourage certain behaviors; understanding their connection to yourself and others begins the reincorporation of your newfound strength.

Be attuned to the simple rule that the inferior function of your type produces specific expressions. In other words, your inferior function shares some general characteristics with those of others of your type; however, the particular expression of it differs according to your history.

Division of the Types

Jung differentiated among the types by identifying the combined attitude and dominant cognitive function (for example, extraverted sensing and introverted thinking). Because the dominant cognitive function directs the overall type, his first division was between the judging (thinking and feeling) and the perceiving (sensing and intuiting) functions. Using this schema, the various types are separated first by the judging function and then by the perceiving function. This difference is profound because it permeates the type and alerts you to the probable inferior—the very cognitive function in the same category that is opposite the dominant (such as extraverted thinking that has an inferior introverted feeling).

On each of the following few pages, you will find a summary of the hallmark qualities of each type followed by a statement concerning the typical compensatory expression of the inferior. These are followed by a brief listing of activities or ideas concerning type development for the inferior.

Keep in mind that the inferior is the least used function. As such, it is the one we are least likely to be aware of when it is expressed. Even those who know type very well find it easier to identify the inferior function of others than to identify expressions of the inferior function in themselves!

The compensatory inferior function may be expressed for a few hours one day, or it may take over for months. If ignored, it grows in strength. Acknowledged and explored, it becomes a new guide.

Please note that we view type behavior as expressions of the habits of mind. We feel using language such as "INFPs act this particular way . . ." to describe a type is a less fluid and more rigid dynamic than experience indicates is reasonable. Therefore, you will at times note that the language used here is different from the usual descriptors of type.

The following descriptions provide a basic outline for the purposes of stimulating study and conversation. Your personal life experience will no doubt alter how you might write a description. These descriptors have the following structure:

    I. Hallmark qualities of type
    II. General descriptors of the compensatory inferior
    III. Activities for inferior function awareness

Compensatory Inferior Descriptions

In the descriptions that follow, we need to remember that the inferior function is simply least consciously active for us. The function is quite active in the unconscious realm, quietly gaining energy and collecting experiences relevant to the function that is involved. As pointed out earlier, there are times we access the least used function to help us address a current situation. But we do not have the active conscious use of this function as we do our most preferred mental habit of Sensing, Intuiting, Thinking, or Feeling. Consequently, there is a considerable amount of independent will our inferior function has as it is least under conscious control.

Ironically, it is when we have lost conscious control through being very tired, extensively stressed, or overconsumption of alcohol that the inferior function will emerge and drive our behavior. It is compensating in two ways. The inferior function is getting its moment in the spotlight to compensate for all its time in the dark world of unawareness. More importantly, however, it is informing you of an imbalance, of a need to compensate for the over extension of your natural strengths and the depletion of your energy. In the vaccum created by this over extension and depletion, the inferior function gets to express itself with considerable magnitude as seen in the following descriptions.

The Judging Types

■

EXTRAVERTED THINKING (ESTJ, ENTJ)

Inferior Function: Introverted Feeling

Typical Extraverted Thinking

Individuals whose typical patterns are Extraverted Thinking are likely to appear analytical and focused on cause-and-effect logic in their outer world. Often methodical and thorough in behavior, Extraverted Thinking directs energy to solving complex problems. Attention is naturally drawn to models and overall goals, with concurrent emphasis on issues of competence and logic.

Typical Compensatory Introverted Feeling

When the inferior function of Extraverted Thinking emerges, it is generally a negative and excessive pattern of overly personal sensitivity. Introverted Feeling in its positive form is characteristically warm and open to concepts and ideas that bring meaning to life. Meaning is found in relationships and loyalties in typical Introverted Feeling ways; however, in its compensatory form, Introverted Feeling is a barbaric and mournful voice demanding to know "What do I live for?"

The feelings of worthlessness are exacerbated by a lack of ability to fully communicate one's feelings. This lack of expression only seems to reinforce the faulty conclusion of incompetence. There is a withdrawal from others as the feelings seem inexplicable. It is as if the self is demanding that you look inward and acknowledge the power of relational values and symbols.

Possible Activities for Type Development

Creative activities that have to do with art, such as drawing symbols or designs that represent feelings or the colors of one's moods, allow the natural Extraverted attitude to access information about the experience. Unlocking the Introverted Feeling energy and giving it life serves both the inferior and the dominant function.

INTRODUCED THINKING (INTP, ISTP)

Inferior Function: Extraverted Feeling

Typical Introverted Thinking

Individuals with a pattern of Introverted Thinking are generally focused on principles and megamodels that explain data, theories, and experience. It seems that the more complex the problem, the more energized these processes become. Criteria, rules of evidence, and verifiable data are major concerns of Introverted Thinking.

Typical Compensatory Extraverted Feeling

In its positive expression, Extraverted Feeling seeks friendship and mutual appreciation. Usually sensitive to rejection or hostility, Extraverted Feeling becomes excited by cooperation and mutuality. In its compensatory form, Extraverted Feeling is driven so hard by the feeling of being disliked that it overwhelms all in the wave of its expression. By virtue of its sticky affection qualities, individuals who see it coming get out of the way.

This moving away by others inadvertently verifies the sense of being unappreciated. The emotions are well out of control for those who prefer Introverted Thinking. This causes anxiety and perhaps even some bitterness at the power of the emotions. By its own nature, compensatory Extraverted Feeling may establish superficial relationships to dispel energy from the inferior function. It is as if the self is demanding recognition of the importance of your passions and how they support your thinking life! You are not just independent but interdependent with others, if you hope to achieve life's goals.

Possible Activities for Type Development

Make an effort to write poetry or some other written expression of the overflow of feelings. Even listing words that express aspects of one's feelings will give life and momentarily capture the experience. By asking a close friend or significant other to see the poetry or word list, ask which expressions capture positive qualities of your relationship. This will ensure that both the basic needs for analysis and affirmation are met. Labeling the feelings is a basic start; specific experiences need to be associated with each label.

EXTRAVERTED FEELING (ESFJ, ENFJ)

Inferior Function: Introverted Thinking

Typical Extraverted Feeling

If ever there were a natural at creating relationships, the Extraverted Feeling expressions are hallmarks for cooperation and personal invitation. Seeking mutuality, Extraverted Feeling shares openly and connects easily with others. Generally, in the face of conflict one strategy of the Extraverted Feeling pattern is to identify the positive qualities or ideas in each person's view.

Typical Compensatory Introverted Thinking

If the typical positive and mature expression of Introverted Thinking is confidence in one's ability to make sense and meaning out of experience, then the compensatory expression of this is a compulsion to find the answer by seeking an expert. This compulsion exists because the compensatory Thinking judgments have been turned on the self, creating considerable self-doubt. This doubt can seemingly only be managed by seeking the sage who will bring an end to the quest for meaning. So critical and negative can the Introverted Thinking voice become that even everyday experience can become twisted.

Social gaffes such as expressing a condolence at a wedding or congratulations at a funeral horrify the Extraverted Feeling. This type of experience reinforces the Introverted Thinking's message that one really is not so competent and capable after all, even in social affairs. It is as if the self is demanding recognition that your thoughts and plans are important; give them more attention and your personal relationships will be enriched!

Possible Activities for Type Development

Identifying accomplishments in one's social life can be a benefit to Extraverted Feeling. Often because it is so natural, active involvement in social activities is not recognized for its contributions to oneself and to others. Making out a report of the week's activities will highlight the distribution of your energy and, if thorough enough, will give you a reminder of the needs of your inner world. A concrete look at how you spend your time will show you if directing some energy toward new and stimulating situations would be feasible. Introverted Thinking wants a plan and wants to know how energy is being used to achieve your life goals.

INTROVERTED FEELING (INFP, ISFP)

Inferior Function: Extraverted Thinking

Typical Introverted Feeling

The general behavioral expression of Introverted Feeling is a passionate conviction to values and commitments. Often quiet and reserved, one typical experience of Introverted Feeling is a deeply rooted adaptability. Generally there is little flash but a great deal of energy put into those activities that are connected to the most deeply held values.

Typical Compensatory Extraverted Thinking

While Extraverted Thinkers are known for their abilities to see many sides of a problem and to rapidly analyze the pros and cons of options, in its negative state Extraverted Thinking becomes a dictator, unyielding and maladaptive. So compulsively reductive and hairsplitting is the compensatory Extraverted Thinking inferior pattern that it can lead to the conclusion that oneself and others around oneself are incompetent.

The obsession with rightness and specificity eventually turns in on the self, unleashing a critical voice that tries to prove how incapable the Introverted Feeling is at taking discernible action. It is as if the self is demanding you to look at the inner map for direction but always stay attuned to the weather outside. Ignore the ability to analyze situations at your own peril; seek clear understanding of alternatives, but evaluate them to your own criteria.

Possible Activities for Type Development

With pencil and paper in hand to record information, discuss with a significant other recent choices you have made. What were the options and the various factors with each choice? Explore the values involved; which seem to emerge at the top of the list? By giving life to those values in written form, you energize your thinking so that the Extraverted function can see the criteria used in the inner world. Extraverted Thinking is less likely to unleash its critical voice when it understands the role that critical values play in feeding the psyche.

The Perceiving Types

■

EXTRAVERTED SENSING (ESTP, ESFP)

Inferior Function: Introverted Intuition

Typical Extraverted Sensing

The hallmark expression of Extraverted Sensing is a firm, concrete, realistic attention to experience. The reliance on sensory experience has rarely failed the Extraverted Sensor; consequently, the Extraverted Sensor is comfortable dealing with current, immediate problems. Energetic and careful in its mature state, the typical Extraverted Sensing function is expressed in skillfully addressing situations, whether they involve people or machines.

Typical Compensatory Introverted Intuition

Rather than experiencing a rich world of interconnections and possibilities, which is common to Introverted Intuitive processes, in the compensatory state this function is filled with dark fantasies and eerie expectations of the future.

The internal awareness is of seeing all the dire possibilities without being able to adequately express feelings or possibilities about them. This difficulty causes some withdrawal from others, for their presence only encourages the inferior function and reinforces the dark feeling of incompetence in social relationships. It is as if the self is demanding that you pay attention to the connection between the concrete reality of life and the more symbolic value that reality may present.

Possible Activities for Type Development

Do something completely different from yesterday's routine. Afterward, intentionally look at how you did it and compare it to yesterday's experience. What are the differences, outcomes, and similarities? Explore the value of the routine and the virtue of a new strategy. What is gained and what is lost? Study the relationship between previous goals and actual accomplishments. The lesson is that a long-range view is useful; today's consequences follow from yesterday's actions. So envisioning several futures provides the possibility that you can begin to consciously decide which future you would prefer, using hunches to get you there.

EXTRAVERTED INTUITION (ENFP, ENTP)

Inferior Function: Introverted Sensing

Typical Extraverted Intuition

Extraverted Intuition expresses itself with a focus on possibilities and innovation. These types are inclined to make connections between experiences and facts. New connections provide new stimulation, which maintains and incites the making of more connections. Connections sometimes add insight and depths to projects already under way. In relationships with either people or ideas, individuals with this pattern look for new ways to enrich their experiences.

Typical Compensatory Introverted Sensing

Mature Introverted Sensing is aware of and enriched by details, but in its compensatory form, details are laden with emotional overtones, perhaps leading to the sensation that a fact or specific awareness establishes and proves a premonition. This can become a compulsion in which the importance of a piece of external evidence or a bodily sensation becomes exaggerated beyond all reasonable concern. Such an excessive focus on a work project or on foods, hygiene, or bodily functions reinforces the unspoken and underlying fear that life is about to take a major turn for the worse. It is as if the self is demanding that you look at the richness around you before leaping to a new precipice. Spend some time developing inside images before seeking new ones.

Possible Activities for Type Development

Use a relaxation exercise and imagine a journey you would like to take. The journey can include images from previous vacations or other actual experiences. Be sure to begin your journey in a dark room and focus on the difficulty of discerning the details of a lightless place; perhaps a room from a childhood experience will create the proper sense of darkness and aloneness. Follow the journey wherever it leads, but be sure you end up in a lighted place, maybe a room you remember as special because of the warm, pleasant memories it evokes. Focus on the details of the experience and enjoy it for your sake.

INTROVERTED INTUITION (INFJ, INTJ)

Inferior Function: Extraverted Sensing

Typical Introverted Intuition

Hallmark expressions of Introverted Intuition are the independent, often individualistic, pursuit of innovation in ideas and activities. Introverted Intuition expresses itself through an inspired understanding of experience. These preferences are often those of individuals who are very interested in theories and models of meaning but willing to splice and remold old theories to accommodate new ideas. Such people are often quite goal-directed and will pursue their ends even if unpopular or unconventional; to them, a difficult challenge means a greater opportunity.

Typical Compensatory Extraverted Sensing

Extraverted Sensing has the natural strength of collecting evidence from the environment—people, things, places. The fluid experience of information enables those using Extraverted Sensing to describe their experiences well. But in its compensatory form, Extraverted Sensing leads to incorrect deductions from a single fact; at times a simple smell can lead to the catastrophic conclusion that a relationship is over. There is no step-by-step logic leading to the conclusion; it is as if the conclusion already existed and merely required the observation of a random fact to allow it to be arrived at.

The consequences of the resulting behavior can make a fool of the Introverted Intuitive. Concerned with competence and possibility, the Introverted Intuitive person is horrified to discover that errors in logic or offenses to others seem to be the order of the day. Further, no explanation for the behavior can be made that is reasonable to others because it was based on a single fact from which an unreasonable conclusion was drawn.

Possible Activities for Type Development

Travel to the nearest art gallery or museum, giving yourself the day to absorb the details of artistic expression. Ask yourself which details stand out in a given piece. See if there is a pattern to the details you select. Go back, view the art again, and purposefully focus on another aspect of the art. See if the piece changes in your perception or if the meaning of the work alters. In this way you can experience in a constructive way the role of detail induction and how focus alters meaning. Also, get involved with crafts and cooking.

INTROVERTED SENSING (ISTJ, ISFJ)

Inferior Function: Extraverted Intuition

Typical Introverted Sensing

The Introverted Sensing pattern of attention produces an accurate and thorough picture of reality, but it may remain unshared. These preferences incline an individual to seek practical rather than new solutions or procedures to problems. Painstaking with details, individuals with the Introverted Sensing pattern care about getting things done on time and according to precise specifications. When carrying out tasks, they will not stop until satisfied that all that could be done has been done. They are consistent and persistent doers.

Typical Compensatory Extraverted Intuition

When the mature functions of Introverted Sensing, which have the natural strengths of clarity and specificity, give way to the inferior, a sinister and pessimistic mood settles on the individual. Events in the impersonal world seem directed as if part of a general plot to destroy one's happiness. A simple phone call from a friend relating some benign recent event may be interpreted as if it were a warning of and precursor to the end of a relationship or some other ghastly state of affairs that is coming soon. People in this state of mind make deductions unsupported by the facts.

The nagging awareness that this is so creates a self-defeating cycle of saying, "Well, look at my bad judgment. I don't have all the facts, but looking at the facts I do have and the kinds of judgments I am making, something bad is bound to happen." Under the circumstances, some minor difficulty proves that the inferior was right and that you are right to feel terrible about your life. It is as if the self is demanding that you look to connections between today and yesterday, and that you plan for possibilities tomorrow.

Possible Activities for Type Development

Work on a hobby or other activity that you haven't worked on for a long time. Visit someone in the hospital, go collect seashells, visit a friend from a long time ago—just do it. It will remind you of your strength and show you that possibilities abound that are neither dire nor foreboding. Some folks report that renting the most sinister movie they can find helps them realize just how much the inferior is playing with their minds.

The Final Word

The inferior function is a natural teacher that reminds you when your energies are depleted, shows you new avenues for development, and can be called upon when the situation demands its gifts. And as teacher, it demands your utmost attention and greatest respect.

It is difficult to respect something that seems foreign to us or at least somewhat at odds with our typical way of responding to those around us. Yet, one may learn to respect something that seems unlikeable if for no other reason than it has a great deal of influence. Take as an example the fact that electric power running through our homes can be helpful and destructive. Its capacity merits our respect and proper treatment. In a similiar fashion, we need to understand that the inferior function can play a positive part in our psychological development. It is present and has a great deal of energy. There are times we can use it as we need it and it expresses itself to allow us to adjust to a situation. But as we pointed out, there are times it emerges out of control. Our capacity to recognize this when it happens and to understand the message that we are in need of adjustment in our daily life is essential for the inferior function to be productive in our lives. If it does nothing more than turn on a mental light that we are working too hard and are ignoring those most important to us, then it is a teacher worth having around.

5

USING THE RUBY SLIPPERS

The Role of Type Development

onsider for a moment *The Wizard of Oz*[32] as a contemporary tale of type development. The story is about a girl, Dorothy, stranded in a strange land on the other side of the rainbow. Because she inadvertently squashes a bad witch upon her arrival, she is granted a pair of ruby slippers by the local good witch.

Viewing the story as a matter of type development (bear with us!), Dorothy is ripped from her frame of reference and sent on a path of discovery (a Sensing process). She meets a scarecrow wanting a brain (Thinking function), a tin man wanting a heart (Feeling function), and a lion wanting courage to face the future (Intuitive function). It requires the unique resources of all the characters to get Dorothy to Oz, where an all-knowing presence—the Wizard—is supposed to be able to return her home and grant her assistants their requests as well. But the Wizard won't help them until they face their fears and struggle against the dark forces that threaten to undo them. When they succeed in doing so, it turns out that the Wizard has no magic; still, he is wise and caring, which enables him to fulfill the desires of Dorothy's companions. Dorothy's own wish, though, is bigger—she wants to go home, and that requires leaving her friends behind to sail in a balloon back over the rainbow, a simple plan foiled by an accident. In the end, she gets home only by submitting to the power of the ruby slippers she had from the beginning of the journey. The moral of the story? There really is no place like home, and the power to get there is with you all the time.

Our Yellow Brick Road

This is an excellent analogy to our own lives. Dorothy's path—the yellow brick road—is like ours: often broken, rarely straight, and featuring no end of characters en route to the desired destination. The story is poignant to us because it is a metaphor for the need to befriend our mental functions one by one and gather them up to successfully complete our life journeys and achieve our goals. These functions, like the new friends Dorothy meets, can contribute to one another and lead to greater wisdom than any could achieve alone. Together, they ultimately overcome formerly unconquerable obstacles. While psychological type is about understanding our habits of perception and judgment, it is also a developmental model. Development implies growth, movement, and evolution. As such, type suggests that there are internal forces that move us toward greater maturity and increased ability to deal with life's challenges. Ultimately, all development is about adjusting and adapting to change while trusting our natural and reliable talents.

Normal individuals move each day toward activities that ensure survival. Whether or not we are conscious of our individual psychologies, how they enable us to adapt and adjust is important; being alive necessitates responding to the stresses and choices that come our way. If we do not adjust, we may suffer serious physical or psychological consequences. Development implies a continually improving capacity to adjust and adapt to environmental demands. The questions psychologists ask often have to do with how, and how consistently within people, such development occurs. You could live a perfectly happy life without knowing anything about psychological models, including psychological type; you could go through life developing your abilities without knowing you have done so. The mechanisms of personal adjustment, change, and adaptation do not require names in order to function, but they still play out.

Patterns Leading to Insights

The beauty of learning human patterns is that we can gain insight into our way of seeing things and responding to life's ups and downs. Because we have the capacity to explore and learn, we can understand our personal and collective psychological development. Perhaps such understanding will enable us to live richer, fuller lives. Knowing how our minds work does not necessarily relieve us from particular stresses, but it may make them more bearable and manageable.

Learning about psychological type as a framework for habits of mind provides us with choices we would not ordinarily have, which means more freedom—any increase in choice is an increase in opportunity. We can come to understand, for example, that even though we may be at our best in situations calling for critique and analysis, we can still learn to be empathetic and accommodating. If we do, we have made a personal advance. As we move down our personal yellow brick roads, we are more likely to enjoy the journey as our range of choices increases. We may not get to Oz any more quickly, but the ability to make conscious choices will ensure that we are more mature and less naive when we get there—and that we have more fun along the way.

Other Developmental Factors

In the same way that a model of the mind's workings such as psychological type is useful, understanding developmental forces within us can be equally practical. For example, if you learn that you are likely to become less physically able with age, you might decide to move into a house with fewer rooms to clean, no lawn to mow, and no stairs to climb. The same is true of psychological changes: If we know they are going to happen, we can be prepared for them. One way of preparing is to understand the three assumptions of development in psychological type: (1) type is part of our mental self-regulation; (2) we specialize, then integrate, mental functions; and (3) development begins within as part of our adaptation to the world outside.

Type as Self-Regulating

One developmental aspect of type is that our minds maintain self-regulating processes that enable us to adapt and respond as our environment changes. Self-regulation means that without effort or even being aware of it, our psychological makeup finds a balance between being active and reflective, having a narrow internal focus and a broad external focus, and so on. In type terms, our minds extravert and introvert, perceive and judge as needed to maintain our general style and sense of well-being.

Self-regulating has to do with keeping internal balances between perception and decision-making, and maintaining the energy distribution between Extraversion and Introversion. For regulation to occur, there must be sources of energy and mental functions that need direction and utilization. As children grow, they begin to test drive their various mental functions, and their preferences emerge very early. For example, some researchers believe that the preference for Extraversion or Introversion appears within the first six months of life.[33] But children, like the rest of us, must internally regulate their preferences; otherwise (for example) a person preferring Extraversion would carry out no Introversion functions, and thus would relentlessly seek experiences without ever giving any thought to what was being experienced. Fortunately, we are equipped for a natural exchange between the two processes. This regulation is true for all of perception and decision making. Like Dorothy in Oz, whose capacities increase as she gains supporting characters, so it is in psychological type, where the proper utilization of the mental functions increases our ability to adjust.

In concrete terms, this simply means that as we go from experience to experience, say English 101 to Math 110, or from the boardroom to the family room, we use different perceptions and decision-making strategies to deal with whatever is presented. English may require us to call on the metaphorical, intuitive side of our imagination, while math may need more specific sensing attention and analytical thinking processes. The boardroom may be the place for decisive, planful, directive action, while the family room may call on the more spontaneous, fluid, go-with-the-flow type of interaction. We change without deliberation if we have already learned what seems most likely to produce a desirable outcome. In other words, we self-regulate our actions, responses, and perceptions.

Type Moves From Specialization to Integration

A second developmental aspect of type is that we develop specialized mental functions before we integrate other mental capacities. Whatever our type, we must be clear and consistent in expressing it before we can gain clarity about other aspects of our personality. The clearer we are about our preference for Extraversion, for example, the more likely we are to be clear when we also use Introversion. An INFP—with Introverted Feeling as the primary process, assisted by Extraverted Intuition—is more likely to know when he is exercising Extraverted Thinking if he is clear about his own type. If we know our habits, it is very clear what habits we don't have. This is a critical aspect of type development: We know our type, are clear about our type, and then we understand the other dimensions of type we can use. But before we can really learn to use these functions in a conscious way, we need to become fully aware of the nature of our own type dynamics—that is, to learn to wear and use our psychological ruby slippers.

The ruby slippers have the power to transform the frame of reference and the quality of life once they are recognized for their natural worth. From the perspective of psychological type, we are more likely to transform our life when we accept our preferences and get on with the business of learning about the appropriate use of the less preferred mental functions. For example, if you are clear about preferring to use Extraverted Sensing to manage your daily challenges, you can use it to seek ways to explore other aspects of your abilities—perhaps your Extraverted Sensing will lead you to a workshop that teaches people to get in touch with their Intuition. Such a workshop fits the need, addresses the natural strength, and provides a door for future development.

We spend a good portion of early life developing our natural preferences, and the second part of life we spend identifying and using other preferences that do not come so easily to our awareness. Some books on midlife change and transition point out that after we spend twenty years or so learning, developing, and adjusting to our work and life partners, we begin to become more aware that time is running out, and so seek out new challenges.[34] We insist on new experiences because we do not want to look back later and regret not exploring or changing when we had the chance. Type assumes that the same processes are at work on the use of mental functions. If we spent the first part of life developing Extraverted Feeling, we may pursue Introverted Thinking activities in the second part—rather like eating fish for twenty years and then developing a hankering for pork.

Type and Adapting to Challenges

As noted above, type theory says we must specialize in a specific pattern of using perception and judgment before we can successfully explore other aspects of mental processes. In a sense, the power of our psychological ruby slippers lies in our type, our home base, our personal framework. Understanding your type offers help on the developmental journey, the destination being to learn when and how to appropriately use those aspects of yourself that you have kept on a mental shelf. Whether or not people know about their psychological types, those who cannot develop clear, appropriate use of their types—who have never experienced being valued or appreciated for the perspective they bring—cannot fully understand or realize their potentials. The two most obvious places a person can be prevented from developing natural expressions are in the family and in school. While conducting career counseling with a young woman, for example, a friend of ours helped her interpret her MBTI inventory. As our friend described the process of Intuition to the client and she confirmed that this was her preferred way of perception, she began to cry. Later the woman said, "You know, this is the first time in my life I have ever felt that anyone understood me. All these years my family and teachers told me I was crazy, and I was about to believe it myself. I have tried and tried to see things their way, but they never once thought it would be worthwhile to try and see things my way. Now I know I am not crazy. It is such a relief." Type gives us a stability of direction to manage the waters of change and to pursue other abilities that might otherwise be ignored. The purpose of this development is to enable us to more wisely address the daily demands of life. What a tragedy when our oars and rudder are taken away just when we start the long journey.

Psychological type would be of little value if it did not provide for our need to adjust to changes and challenges in life. If we are good students, then we learn from previous experiences and use those lessons in addressing similar situations. Type reminds us of the attention we pay to situations and the conclusions on which we can act. Type suggests that the things that frightened us at age twenty may be used to our advantage at age forty. For example, if you were afraid of making logical, orderly—Extraverted Thinking—presentations in the early part of your career, chances are that in order to advance, you learned to do it anyway. Healthy individuals learn to use those aspects that increase their likelihood of achieving success.

Jung proposed that as we grow older, our internal psychological mechanisms demand challenge and opportunity. Like a tulip bulb that knows when to grow and unfold, our internal psychological processes stimulate change of their own accord and timing. Those who prefer Intuition may find themselves passionate about a Sensing-related hobby in their thirties, for example, because it allows for the expression of the nonpreferred perception without threatening the more basic preference.

Other Developmental Models

To understand the significance of type as a developmental model, we need to recognize that type is different from other developmental perspectives. Other models assume that human development occurs in a relatively sequential manner, moving from simple to complex behaviors. Further, development at a later stage requires competence at an earlier stage. For example, you can learn to walk only after you have learned to crawl.

By contrast, type does not assume sequential development. Type is like the inner veins of a tree, influential and essential to growth but allowing it to occur in any direction in response to the environment. Further, though type does not assume the sequential, hierarchical development of preferences, it does presume that human behavior is quite complex and serves many purposes.

What We Have Learned

In somewhat practical terms, type development is about what we have learned to do and what we have avoided learning to do. For example, those who have a natural preference for Extraverted Thinking and have learned this way of making decisions quite well are less likely to have used or developed Extraverted Feeling. Being comfortable as verbal, analytical, systematic problem solvers, they act that way more often than not and gain reinforcement for it more often than when they express themselves in other ways. Thus, they may tend to simply ignore Extraverted Feeling throughout life.

But type development is the process of activating those previously unacknowledged functions, learning their capabilities, and using them in appropriate ways. So if you spent the first half of life enhancing your natural patterns of perception and judgment, you will develop more completely when you work on the less used patterns. Learning when to appropriately use your nonpreferred mental functions and to use them well is the goal. It is the same as the medicine wheels of the Plains Indians mentioned in the Preface. Life's journey is one of growing awareness of, appreciation for, and skill in using expressions outside your natural view. When you gain this ability, you earn the privilege of placing a new stone in your wheel. Those who meet you and observe your understanding of many perspectives will know that you are truly wise.

Much of the literature on adult development focuses on the important tasks of growing up, selecting a career and a mate, being creative in one's work, and making choices about the contributions to be made later in life. Additional adult development material is focused on physical and mental changes. There is very little on the personal, inner psychological work we must do to move successfully through life. In many regards, psychological type theory gives the largest scope of mental development of any current model.

Learning From Experiences

Some of the most interesting work on adult development is emerging around research on the lessons people learn from their various life experiences.[35] The assumptions guiding this work are that we are attracted to those things we do well and avoid those things that we believe we do not do well. Through our adult life we select experiences and challenges that we feel reasonably able to accomplish. As we get older, it becomes increasingly clear that the experiences we avoided at an earlier time would have taught valuable lessons that could be very useful now. Thus, we strive to excel at our strengths, but we avoid confronting our weaknesses until it is absolutely necessary to do so in order to continue to achieve greater levels of satisfaction.

For example, if you graduate from college with a degree in industrial engineering, chances are you pursue a job with a firm that needs an entry-level industrial engineer. Assuming you are generally able and ambitious, you receive promotions and excel at the work the company needs you to perform. One day, however, you are promoted to supervisor. Within a few months, you wish you had taken the human relations courses you pooh-poohed in college and the professional development workshops you avoided early in your career, because now you need insights regarding motivational and leadership skills. Having assiduously avoided such soft topics to pursue expertise in engineering, you are now woefully unprepared to tackle supervisory tasks, and further success may depend on learning things now that you could have easily learned earlier. But you quickly set about learning these skills and vow that you will not get caught like this again. Assuming that you do learn the necessary skills to supervise, and you perform very well, you are now promoted to a position as unit manager. While the lessons of leading and supervising those with less experience or expertise were difficult enough, you now need the ability to persuade peers and make public presentations to upper management and clients. If you have not prepared for such a day, you may once again wish you had learned earlier the skills needed now for this new challenge.

Echoes of Type Development

This model of lessons learned and lessons avoided has a very strong parallel in type development. Type theory says that type preference is part of the reason we are attracted to specific interests and activities, and that these are reinforced by a sense of accomplishment. Later, we have to learn things about ourselves that we had ignored in order to maintain a healthy view of the world.

We suspect that, as more researchers explore the processes of adult development and move beyond looking solely at the tasks of development, these basic principles of type will be supported. After more than two decades of asking questions about type development to thousands of program participants, we have enough evidence to suggest that type development is a very real and powerful force in adult growth. It is clear to us that, properly understood, type can aid adults throughout their lives in making more conscious choices and in avoiding the blind spots that can plague us.

In adult life we constantly strive for effectiveness—for the ability to produce results. We want to be effective as partners, parents, associates, managers, and in any other role we can imagine. We want our needs to be understood and satisfied through our engagement in relationships, work, parenting, and all the other roles we choose. If we decide to be parents, we generally want our kids to grow up to be happy, healthy, successful individuals. If these things happen, we think of ourselves as effective. When we prepare a presentation for work, we do our best to design it to be effective. Electricians want to put in the wiring, switches, and outlets in such a way that power is safely distributed in a structure, and if they do so they think of themselves as effective.

Developing Efficacy

Often we are effective because we have sought experiences that will give us the abilities to do the job, or we model our effort after someone who has done the job well (parents, for example, usually do not go to parenting school but rely on their observations of other parents, especially their own). What we really want is more than effectiveness; we want efficacy. Efficacy means making more conscious choices and actions based on the use of all of our capacities rather than merely acting out of routine. Efficacy is the awareness and use of our skills, our knowledge, and the limits of our capabilities. It is the belief that no matter what comes our way, we can adapt, adjust, and develop a strategy to respond. So the ultimate end of type development—like Dorothy's use of the ruby slippers—is efficacy: consciously using our powers to get us where we want to go.

To explore the development of the sixteen types, table 12 provides two descriptions for each type. The first is a description of qualities of those people who are clear about their types and who have been observed as being effective in using the behaviors that result from their types. The second is a description of the qualities needed to obtain greater efficacy. To increase your own efficacy, you might ask others who know you well what kinds of things you could do to learn new behaviors, to respond differently, and to immerse yourself in new ways of getting things done. The intent behind listing in table 12 some activities and ideas to consider is merely to give you hints and trends; these are by no means prescriptive or comprehensive.

Developed Types

The following descriptions give you our best handle on the home base—the natural psychological ruby slippers. They are followed by the qualities that type needs to develop in order to achieve efficacy in later life. Keep in mind that these are the actual words used by individuals to describe their own types and their observations of other types.

As we move through our daily chores, we make decisions to behave in ways that reinforce who we are and that support things about which we feel positive. We have a system for noting benchmarks in life—entering college, graduating, first job, marriage, and so on—but we rarely make note of the changes that occur quietly in our minds. Adjustments we make, lessons we learn, actions we take today that we would not have taken earlier are signs of significant internal events. In much the same way, each individual's psychological type undergoes change and transition.

Type unfolds and develops of its own accord; in supportive conditions it grows and blossoms, contributing to self-esteem and to the lifelong paths each of us make. Like Dorothy in Oz, we move down the road of life, and if we are attentive to the lessons of experience we activate energies and talents that enable us to face

TABLE 12

TYPE PATTERNS IN ADULT DEVELOPMENT

ISTJ

Introverted Sensing With Extraverted Thinking

When developed Pragmatic, detail oriented, consistent, rely on past experiences, concise, focused, serious, orderly, methodological, practical, decisive, reserved, predictable, organized, realistic, takes time to get to know them, trust facts, want and make structure, conscientious, calm, make time to be alone, hard to dissuade once mind is made up, responsible, energized by data

For efficacy Learn to trust the inner voice and the intuition of others, create opportunities for complete freedom from closure, learn multiple decision making models, engage two or three more people in problem solving than you normally would

ISFJ

Introverted Sensing With Extraverted Feeling

When developed Organized, succinct communicators, want thorough understanding of facts before acting, service oriented, enjoy helping others, careful, reliable, realistic, concise

For efficacy Seek opportunities to let go; immerse yourself in activities such as art classes or philosophy debates at a local university, get involved with psychologically minded programs, join a book club

difficult challenges and respond appropriately to them. In normal circumstances, we come equipped to manage life and adjust to its daily demands. But we are rarely comfortable settling just for clarity about our capabilities at the moment; we want to become more, to exceed current expectations. The urge to move on, to seek new challenges, to squeeze more from life comes from within. Type theory tells us that the journey down the road of life can be made intelligently and with awareness of who we are and what we can become. And in learning new lessons and developing new capabilities, we never leave behind our natural strengths; in fact, we may enhance them through our acceptance of new opportunities.

TABLE 12 (CONTINUED)

TYPE PATTERNS IN ADULT DEVELOPMENT

INTJ

Introverted Intuition With Extraverted Thinking

When developed   Play out conversations in their heads, like planned changes, like new challenges, reflective, independent, see the big picture, oriented to the future, determined, purposeful, resourceful, ask why, hard-driving, relentless about precision, use principles for decision making

For efficacy   Commit regularly to a social help volunteer organization, seek out others who share many of your qualities but have achieved success in very different ways from you, engage in group training programs with a physical component (such as rafting) to drive focus on the moment

INFJ

Introverted Intuition With Extraverted Feeling

When developed   Quiet problem solvers, global perspective, avoid conflict, like many points of view, enjoy generating options, work with complex people problems, establish enduring friendships, decisive, attentive to other people

For efficacy   Identify physical and social activities which challenge your world view and require you to live explicitly in the moment, attend training programs on giving and receiving feedback and promptly implement the training, develop a regular time for selected activities

In a sense, type development is the process of moving up a spiral of ever-increasing awareness of, and capacity to use, our mental processes of perception and judgment. We circle about our most central part as we move up the spiral, and if we are in tune with our growth it will affirm T. S. Eliot, who wrote:

Time past and time future
What might have been and what has been
Point to one end, which is always present
We will not cease from our exploration
And the end of all our exploring will be to arrive
Where we started
And know the place for the first time.[36]

TABLE 12 (CONTINUED)

TYPE PATTERNS IN ADULT DEVELOPMENT

ISTP

Introverted Thinking With Extraverted Sensing

When developed Logical, factual, focus on what is relevant to here and now, constantly analyzing, often seen as detached, thorough, practical-minded problem solvers, highly value independence

For efficacy Seek opportunities which require brainstorming and long-term project management with others, regularly engage in personal planning about goals for the next ten years, attend seminars about trends for the future, pursue marriage- or relationship-enrichment seminars, groups, or similar short-term experiences

---
INTP

Introverted Thinking With Extraverted Intuition

When developed Love problem solving, complexity, and new ideas; analytical, build mental models, like to synthesize ideas, strive for objectivity, like problem solving as exploration, avoid small talk, want specific and direct feedback, constant gatherers of information, impersonal, tolerant, seen as critical

For efficacy Attend seminars on relationship development such as marriage- or relationship-enrichment workshops, develop frequent opportunities for feedback from the folks you work with, get involved in community or social projects, complete a group survival program in a wilderness area

TABLE 12 (CONTINUED)

TYPE PATTERNS IN ADULT DEVELOPMENT

ISFP

Introverted Feeling With Extraverted Sensing

When developed   Pride in self-control, seek affiliation, use orderly ways to nurture others, careful about facts, reflective about current situations, seen as quiet and introspective, express commitment and appreciation in specific terms

For efficacy   Volunteer to lead a social help group, develop contacts in professions very different from your own, seek feedback on problem-solving style, attend project management and problem solving seminars, look for non-work-related hobbies

INFP

Introverted Feeling With Extraverted Intuition

When developed   Reserved, intense, passionate about values, like to facilitate discussion, seek harmony, dislike being caught off guard, enjoy autonomy, genuine about values, go with the flow, stealth risk takers, often the social conscience in a group, inner directed, perfectionistic, oriented toward causes, relentless searchers for what is meaningful, intrigued by complexity, prefer win/win situations

For efficacy   Seek seminars in forecasting and trend analysis, take lessons in public speaking and debate, try out for community theater roles, attend local business forums, annually develop a five-year plan, learn several conflict management techniques

TABLE 12 (CONTINUED)

TYPE PATTERNS IN ADULT DEVELOPMENT

ESTP

Extraverted Sensing With Introverted Thinking

When developed   Energetic seekers of experiences, get caught in the moment, keep communication brief, decide by talking, outgoing, meet deadlines just in time, seen as forceful and excitable

For efficacy   Take time for regular periods of quiet and reflection in which you purposefully avoid describing in detail what happened in various situations but make general lists of their possible meanings, take leadership of a six- to eight-month project, pursue retreat opportunities in varied physical environments

ESFP

Extraverted Sensing With Introverted Feeling

When developed   Enjoy amusement and physical play, active, resourceful when dealing with people, focus on the immediate, find the easy way to do hard things, low need for closure, like to solve conflict as a go-between, curious about social interactions, like nature, usually can give the facts of a situation

For efficacy   Take courses or seminars in conflict management, seek opportunities to work with people more technically trained than yourself on selected projects, write in a journal about personal reactions to people and situations, develop contacts with people in hobbies and activities which are very different from your natural interests

TABLE 12 (CONTINUED)

TYPE PATTERNS IN ADULT DEVELOPMENT

ENFP

Extraverted Intuition With Introverted Feeling

When developed Involved with many different tasks, work in short intense spurts of energy, insatiable curiosity, love creating ideas, trust others at face value, diplomatic, difficulty deciding, trust hunches, exuberant, spontaneous, accommodating, challenge systems and rules, take pride in adapting to situations, insightful about people and their needs, easygoing, warm, work well under pressure, optimistic, good at reading between the lines

For efficacy Seek several short-term projects which require attention to financial, operational, and service tasks; seek individual performance hobbies which are completed with a group (such as watercolor painting classes), find opportunities to focus on specific experiences such as group problem solving on a local historic district issue

ENTP

Extraverted Intuition With Introverted Thinking

When developed Value change, like to learn, avoid routines, take risks, future-oriented, slow to trust, verbally critical, think while talking, eclectic, make changes often, quick-thinking, love ideas and intellectual challenge, ingenious, adventurous, questioning, defiant, delegate the details, like a quick pace

For efficacy Engage in physical routines with a conscious focus on what, why, when, how, where, and who; make a year-long commitment to a social service volunteer agency, take courses in project management with an engineering bent to the topics, develop networks in service-oriented businesses for comparisons

TABLE 12 (CONTINUED)

TYPE PATTERNS IN ADULT DEVELOPMENT

ESTJ

Extraverted Thinking with Introverted Sensing

When developed   Competitive, want completed jobs to be done right, organized, direct, frank, sense of urgency, high energy, seek and
make decisions, reliable, outspoken, matter-of-fact orientation, develop pragmatic skills, results-oriented, expressive
of critical analysis

For efficacy   Attend collaboration training, find opportunities to develop
creative writing skills (stressing, for example, motivation,
vision, global systems), ask for a project which requires
careful and moderately slow analytical processes, pursue
community involvement in agencies and programs which
require individual rather than group problem solving

ENTJ

Extraverted Thinking With Introverted Intuition

When developed   Reasoned, logical, curious, fair with high expectations, like
to control, focused on the future, organized, logical action
takers, seek variety, energetic about many topics and interests, like immediate planning, persistent, pursue closure,
want to have fairness in relationships, motivated by challenges

For efficacy   Put yourself on task forces that deal with issues only tan-
gentially related to your main work, develop relationships
with those who appear to feel best about addressing individual needs rather than working on systems problems,
identify as many relationship and people outcomes as
financial or achievement outcomes from working on projects, tasks, or selected jobs

TABLE 12 (CONTINUED)

TYPE PATTERNS IN ADULT DEVELOPMENT

ENFJ

Extraverted Feeling with Introverted Intuition

When developed Warm, friendly, empathetic, lively, approachable and initiating, doers, flexible, want to be trusted, like humor, sensitive to criticism, enjoy innovating and acting on new ideas, want others to be comfortable, bridge builders among people, try to make others feel important

For efficacy Volunteer to help organize and deliver services in a health-related social service, attend seminars on critical thinking and scientific problem-solving methods, develop hobbies which rely on spontaneous responses, seek regular discussions with individuals who successfully manage conflict to review the strategies they use

ESFJ

Extraverted Feeling With Introverted Sensing

When developed Committed and dedicated to others, respectful, nurturing, active listeners, enjoy a variety of people, organized, give attention to details related to people, talkative, sympathetic, tactful, realistic, radiate sympathy, motivated by appreciation, orderly in small matters, often seen as gregarious

For efficacy Attend abstract, intellectually loaded seminars on financial topics, participate in local debate clubs, identify and network with individuals involved with theoretical topics or imaginative endeavors (such as art, music, or theater), find three or four opportunities each week to meditate

PATHWAYS OF COMMUNICATION

Type as a Lantern on the Path to Understanding

livia Pearman, four years old at the time, asked her dad Roger (coauthor of this book) a simple question: "When do I get to be a person?" Shocked, he began to wonder where he had gone wrong. After years of training in psychology and education, staying home to raise his infant children, and spending untold hours focused on his daughter's development, her question seemed unthinkable. How could she doubt she was a person? Bending down to look his daughter in the face, tears welling in his eyes, he asked, "What do you mean, Olivia?" She said, "When do I get to make decisions that count?" Roger asked again, "What do you mean? What kinds of decisions would you like to make?" Olivia, looking him straight in the eye, replied, "I want a calendar and a clock!"

Roger immediately understood. She had heard him make appointments and schedule meetings, so this must be what real people do—they get to use calendars and clocks! So father and daughter got in the car, drove to the nearest store, and selected a clock and calendar. Olivia still uses them daily.

This illustrates the communication process with which we all live. A person gives us information, and we associate certain meanings to it depending on our own experience. Until we ask the person who sent the message, however, we cannot be sure what it really means. The swift and fluid interchange that we euphemistically call communication creates both the bridges and the chasms between human beings. The simple task of exchanging ideas, information, or experience so that each person knows what the other really means turns out to be a rather complex business.

To fully understand this complexity, we must begin with the proposition that a successful communicator can communicate regardless of his or her own gender, race, age, and culture, or those of the audience. Of course, these factors influence how we communicate because they affect how certain words and expressions are interpreted. Successful communication depends on taking the time to establish and agree upon certain common experiences and common interpretation of those experiences. When Olivia initiated communication with her father, each had very different experiences in mind when using the phrase "to be a person." Only when Roger took the time to find out what Olivia meant—to reach an agreement with her about the experience they were discussing— did a satisfactory outcome for the interaction become possible. The expression of information, a critical part of this dynamic, is heavily influenced by a person's psychological type and by what the person has learned.

What We All Want

Whatever the job, situation, or relationship, we all face the problems and pleasures of communication. From our research and that of many other experts in the field, and from our own personal experiences, we feel comfortable asserting that there are certain qualities in communication that most reasonable, interpersonally healthy people want to experience when they interact with others.

First, we generally want people to be trustworthy and to perceive us as being trustworthy. We also want honesty from others and the space and security within a relationship to be more honest. We want few barriers built and a joint commitment to remove any existing barriers. We want to hear from others about those things that truly interest them, and in turn we want to experience interest from others. Finally, we want to have our communication treated as it was intended—specifically, we want it understood that our constructive problem solving is not a personal attack. As illustrated in the opening example, this wish list in communication does not always fit so easily within our communication processes. Just when we think we have given a message of trust, we learn that it has been received with doubt; when we have tried to communicate a description, we learn it was heard as slanted in favor of a particular view; when we tried to keep silent so that another would have space to speak of his life's interests, we learn we were perceived as dull and uninterested.

The trick is to learn to communicate in such a way as to keep the flow of information "clean." This means being aware of how we express our thoughts and ideas as well as becoming aware of how others may express themselves.

Psychological Type as a Handle

Psychological type gives us a handle on how healthy, normal individuals usually interpret and express themselves about events. Though type preferences are not all there is to the communication equation, understanding the concepts of type provides an excellent start toward making the most of our efforts. Psychological type will give us these insights if we can begin to understand the basic elements of attention and decision making. When efforts are made to communicate, type offers us a path toward greater understanding of people and their probable intentions. Because it is part of the fabric of everyday life, psychological type provides a rational way for individuals to reach agreement about a shared experience.

Our typical patterns of attending to and deciding about information affect everything about the way individuals are attracted to, interpret, and eventually attempt to express their responses to experiences. Type furnishes us with a model for understanding those patterns; it gives us a different ear for listening and a different voice for sharing our thoughts and feelings, and helps us gain a new perspective on some of the most difficult aspects of misunderstandings in communication.

We Are Always Communicating Messages

We must accept that, in the presence of others, we are always communicating messages, all the time. We have no exit, no reprieve from the awareness of another person. You can convey the message "leave me alone" or "you seem interesting" to total strangers in a theater line without a word ever being spoken. Whether you intend it or not, if another person believes you sent a message, then you have. You could be minding your own business in an elevator when a dust mote irritates your contact lens. Completely unaware of those around you, you breathe a sigh, wink and roll the irritated eye heavenward, all the while twitching your face in search of relief. This arouses empathy in one fellow passenger who herself is aggravated by lingering smoke in the elevator and attributes your behavior to the same. But another passenger experiences disdain and some anxiety about riding in an elevator with someone so disturbed as to have lost control of his facial muscles. He noticed the office sign of a criminal psychologist in the building and is wondering if you are a client. Both leave your presence confident they have understood something about you, yet neither one realized that your contact lens was the source of it all. In some situations you could be perceived as acting like a criminal; in the preconceived notions of the observer, you have been understood. The movie *Twelve Angry Men* gives a wonderful depiction of this very process.[37]

Projection Is at the Heart of It

In general terms, the word *projection* is used in psychology when discussing unconscious scripts that are brought to life on—projected onto—external circumstances. For example, if after meeting a person you begin to feel this person is unacceptable and unlikable, and if there is no basis for the feeling, you are likely to be experiencing a projection based on qualities about yourself that you dislike. When you perceive those same unacceptable qualities in the other person, your unconscious mind sees that projection (watches that movie, if you will) and swiftly informs you that you do not like that person.[38] All of this goes on unconsciously, making it difficult to immediately recognize or address.

A classic example might be the person already a bit aggravated about having to do housekeeping who suddenly trips over his spouse's shoe in the middle of the floor. In a fit of self-righteousness, he marches out of the room to confront her over her slovenliness but finds himself face down on the floor, toes throbbing—he's tripped over another shoe, this one his own! Part of his irrational anger over a simple shoe left on the floor is really anger at recognizing his own behavior and seeing how unattractive it is. But projection has a broader meaning than just seeing your own habits in others—it is at the core of all interactional dynamics.

Projection in this context means that each of us takes the words we hear and the actions we see and overlays our own experiences on them. For example, the word *fish* may prompt some to remember fishing by a lake, others to imagine visiting an aquarium, and still others to think about eating at a seafood restaurant. We hear the word and immediately put our experience on it. Unless we ask the speaker for more information, our projection may give an entirely different meaning than what was intended.

Projection is a useful term because it implies connecting experience and emotion in such a way as to create meaning. *Association* and *recognition* are not the same as projection; they imply somewhat more cognitive and conscious processes. Projection is the unconscious process whereby individuals create meaning about their experiences, especially in interactions. Note, however, that the same process is at work when we are quietly alone reflecting on ideas, comments, or experience. Projection is happening whenever we are faced with experiences, be they inter-personal interactions among people or purely one-way interactions, as when reading a book, watching television, walking on the beach, or seeing a play. Projection is not always negative—far from it. It simply exists, and it must be understood if there is any hope of improving our communications.

Prejudice, Preconception, and Emotional Reactions: The Result of Projection Gone Awry

Misunderstanding Is More Than Word Confusion

Communication usually becomes an issue when there is a misunderstanding. As we have illustrated, sometimes the misunderstanding relates to the words or the tone used. More often than not, when conflict occurs due to miscommunication, we fear there is something deeper. Because of the intensity of these conflicts, it is important to find a neutral and constructive model for unraveling them. Type is such a model, and by first looking at the primary sources of misunderstanding, we can plainly see the usefulness of type in communication.

Prejudice, preconception, and emotional reactions are the opposite sides of the coins of appreciation, acceptance, and positive feelings that result from projections. Prejudice, preconception, and emotional reactions are the sources of misunderstanding. Prejudice, the irrational judgment of other people or situations, leads to stereotyping. We project our questions and doubts about a whole group onto any individual from that group whom we encounter. It is as if all the unique attributes of individuals within a specified group have been lumped into a chemist's beaker and cooked out; only a hard and lifeless residue remains, obstructing the flow of information, ideas, and events so that real dialogue can never take place.

Preconception, the assumption of what will be, leads to our paying attention to only the information that supports our presumed truth. Preconception is a self-congratulatory attitude that assumes rightness and knowledge. When a new situation bears any similarity to previous experience, we project our earlier learning onto it with unshakable certitude. Then, because we think we know what's going on, we stop attending to any new information that could dissuade us. Sleight-of-hand artists rely on this habit in audiences to create their illusions.

Emotional reactions are those gut responses to events that bend our rationality like a prism bends light. This distortion compromises our usual reliance on factual information to the point where the rules of fair play often become swords of righteousness. Negative emotional reactions are often the result of old, unconscious fears being projected onto new situations. For example, after a childhood of being taunted about being chubby, a father may respond emotionally and withdraw his son from the soccer team when the coach makes an offhand remark about flabby kids needing to do more work.

These three—prejudice, preconception, and emotional reactions—are repeatedly at the heart of miscommunicated information.

Type Offers a New Language for Communicating With the World

Today, an awareness of the interdependent nature of the world calls for a new way of communication. Certainly wars still exist—more than a hundred at any given time around the globe, on average—and these are a stark reminder that ancient prejudice, preconception, and emotionality are still quite strong and compelling in human behavior. But we know now that distant wars have local consequences; our interdependent economies require a confrontation with the fact that we cannot escape communicating with those who are different. As we work through these ideas, it becomes clear that psychological type offers a constructive way to communicate and to understand communication within our own culture and across cultures. Type shows us new ways to speak and new ways to listen, but learning any new way of communication requires patience, awareness of communication mechanisms, and a willingness to be open to new insights. The insights of psychological type inform us both of the ways we misunderstand and of the ways we may eventually communicate more constructively. Type teaches us to apply the old carpenters' rule—measure twice, cut once—to interactions. In other words, we must be very sure what other people mean when they use a given word or phrase, and only take action after we've reached a mutual understanding.

Through development of a mature understanding of our own processes and of the complexity of life, we are able to escape the narrow confines of the boundaries cast by prejudice, preconception, and emotionality. But to bring light to the darkness inherent to unconscious processes, we must be willing to expose them, recognize them, integrate them, and move on to develop other parts of ourselves. Our emergence and our struggle throughout life is to specialize, to become so good at what we do that we do it with grace and ease. One outcome of this emergence, of this specialization, is the further development of type preferences and behaviors.

Preferences Lead to Focus

Preferences for left- or right-handedness, for certain colors, for certain foods all serve the individual. These preferences allow for specialization, for focus. In the same way, psychological type is the by-product of preferences and habits of mind that mold our expressions. In the first part of this book, we argued that psychological type is another example of the evolution of the human psyche. As basic as collecting energy, sorting perceptions, and making judgments may be, these are the mechanisms that forge, among many human qualities, our prejudices, preconceptions, and emotions.

An Argument

The scenario: Two men are having an argument. One is very tough-minded, logical, impersonal, objective, and arrogant. The other is very accommodating, responsive, personal, and somewhat subservient. Their differences are so striking that they seem funny.

The action: Suddenly, the second man hits and knocks out the arrogant logician. Everyone applauds the gentle man for putting the other down, but he is filled with remorse for harming another human being and departs, returning with a gift and an apology for his victim. However, the tough man states that he was satisfied that they had settled the issue like men. He rejects the other's "pity" and protests the insult. Stunned, the accommodating character leaves, stuttering, disoriented, and disbelieving that his motive could be so misunderstood.

The explanation: Though not delivered here with clever dialogue and exaggerated antics, this scene from a recent situation comedy captures a number of very important issues in communication. The interpersonal styles of the characters are so very different that they are disgusted with one another. It did not appear that the events of the scene should lead to violence and misunderstanding, but when both men unwittingly projected their various meanings onto the events the result was virtually inescapable. We constantly live out the idea that what we believe to be true actually is true—our perceptions become our realities—and as rational human beings we take action based on reality. Because each perceived the other as the enemy, both men generated a great deal of emotional heat between them. The fight is perceived by one as the just settlement of their disagreement, while the other sees it as a demoralizing event. The gift is a peace offering to the one giving it, pity to the recipient. These two men were both raised in the same culture, even attended the same schools, but are as different as people from separate countries. They do not see the world the same way. Messages were sent but not received in the manner in which they were intended.

Our Precarious Balance

As in the sitcom scene, there is a precarious balance in every interaction. Whether we like it or not, we are sending messages all the time. Some we intend; others we are unaware of. Most projections are created by integrating verbal contents, tone, emotional expression, appearance, and delivery. Simply being in a room with another person is going to send a message, so learning how to appropriately direct the message is very important. We make a serious error when we assume that the person we are talking to is indeed receiving the exact message we intended to send.

Useful Utterances

Every day we assume our utterances are understood. Like the habits of mind that make up our psychological type, we unconsciously assume people know what we mean when we are sharing information. By watching how people respond to or act on our words, we get feedback that the message was received and understood. But what of the messages from which we get no feedback?

What aspects of our communication style trigger another's reaction that leads to a misunderstanding? How about our interpretation of others' messages? How often do we check them out? How aware are we of our own reactions and how these reactions affect our judgments?

Fortunately, psychological type can help us unravel these issues and encourage us to develop a constructive interpersonal style that avoids unnecessary misunderstandings, and possibly a few broken noses! For if communication begins with internal projection, we need to know what signals are hitting the screen, so to speak. Psychological type suggests that we can identify, understand, and constructively utilize differences among the types in communication patterns. Through type we can get a handle on some of the typical prejudices, preconceptions, and emotional "buttons" of most people. In short, we have a pathway to understand the kinds of images and associations different types make with experiences which in turn lead to the projection of meaning in communication. So we have a cycle: We project what we learn, we learn from what we are, we are at least partly the outcome of the preferences we live out in daily life—and the way we live feeds what we learn. And so it goes, on and on.

If, for example, we learn at an early age that people are to be mistrusted and treated with suspicion, we tend to see others' behaviors as having bad intentions and ulterior motives. Consequently, we withhold information from people and protect ourselves in ways that are likely to elicit responses that support our suppositions. If our preference is for Extraversion, we may express our distrust energetically; if we are Introverted, we may simply become too anxious around others to engage them. In either case, the results are the same: We project certain meaning onto another person's behavior, behave ourselves in a way that supports our assumptions, and receive confirmation that our projection was correct.

Obviously relationships are never this simple, and the cycle is often transformed. This usually comes about through people changing their projections. One way this occurs is by observing others and seeing the outcomes of their different behavior. Another is when the process and projections are exposed and individuals look at their behavior and decide to change it. Bringing light to the darkness, as Jung put it, is a difficult process but very productive for personal growth and relationship enrichment.[39]

What We Learn

To enrich the communication cycle, we must first acknowledge we are in it, identify other ways to react, and consciously seek those lessons we have avoided. For example, if you have avoided learning about communication skills because you thought they were soft disciplines, chances are you think of yourself as tough-minded and are drawn to things that reinforce your perception. You would certainly be startled if, after twenty years of marriage, your spouse were to say that communication with you has been nearly impossible, and then leaves as a result. Whatever lessons we avoid along the way usually only become more costly lessons later. So if only for efficiency's sake, as you study the following pages on the communication issues of the sixteen types and again in chapter 7 when valuing differences is explored, you might ask yourself what lessons you have been avoiding.

In the pages ahead we look at the general communication style of each of the preferences and then of the sixteen whole types. We reflect on the lessons each is drawn to, and on those typically avoided in communications with others. Before we can see the positive contributions of those whose preferences are different from our own, we must first understand the component parts and then the dynamic whole of each type. Understanding, however, is not the same as valuing; this issue is covered in the next chapter.

What We Are

So far, we have asserted that: (1) when two or more people are together, communication is an ongoing fact, whether we are trying to send messages or not; (2) projection is at the root of all communication—we hear or see something and project our meaning onto it; (3) most misunderstandings occur because of prejudice, preconception, and emotional reactivity, which are opposite the honesty, candor, and openness we generally want in relationships; (4) how we express ourselves, what we project, and part of our prejudices, preconceptions, and emotional reactions are related to our psychological type; (5) psychological type can help us rationally understand our expressions and projections in constructive ways, and can also help us listen to others more effectively.

Remembering that type is all about how we usually attend to information, what we attend to, how we decide, and how we act on what we believe to be true, we will explore type's contribution to communication first by exploring the preferences singularly and then by studying the more important and complex effects of type dynamics.

As a refresher, note the following dimensions from the MBTI personality inventory, which is based on Jung's theory:

Extraverting	Seeking and initiating in the environment
Introverting	Receiving and reflecting on the environment
Sensing	Attraction to data from present-oriented experiences, often seeking pragmatic and realistic information
Intuition	Attraction to ideas about future possibilities, seeing patterns, seeking abstract and theoretical information
Thinking	Deciding by logical arguments; often critical and analytical
Feeling	Deciding by value, relational arguments; often accommodating
Judging	Acting in a decisive way, either in an analytical or a value-oriented way
Perception	Acting in an emergent, go-with-the-flow way; primarily conscious of either the present or the imagined future

Communication Effects of Extraversion/Introversion

By habit, Extraverts tend to express themselves freely. They are so comfortable initiating in their environment that they assume everyone else is, too. Further, a lack of immediate reaction from Extraverts usually occurs when they do not trust a situation (or person) or when they feel incapable of making a reasonable response. Aware of this personal discomfort, they often assume that when they see someone else who is not immediately responsive, or who appears cautious, then that person must also be uncomfortable, worried, and possibly slow or only moderately competent in the situation.

Notice the ease with which the Extravert's experience becomes the baseline for judging others' reactions. This is the nature of projection. It is an unconscious process that colors our understanding. It may well be the Extravert's first unspoken prejudice; understanding is based on what the Extravert is comfortable with, rather than what may be true for an Introvert.

For example, a consultant we know had been working with a group of managers on a regular basis over several months. On a break during one session, the supervisor of the group approached with a smug grin and said, "You know, John, I've finally figured out why I don't trust people like you!" Somewhat taken aback, John nonetheless remembered his own lessons well enough to ask, "What do you mean by that?" The supervisor said, "I've been watching you for all these months now, and I've finally figured it out. Whenever one of my managers asks you a question, you always pause before you respond. I can see the gears turning in your head, and your not responding immediately tells me you're withholding information from my people. I don't trust anyone who doesn't tell me all they know." This was all John needed to understand what was going on. He said, "George, if I ask you a question and you pause before responding, could I trust your response as being the whole truth?" George replied quickly, "Absolutely not. If I can't answer immediately, that means I have a hidden agenda to sort through before I can formulate a verbal response." "Aha!" John said. "Just because that's true for you doesn't mean it is for me. Remember our sessions on type a few months ago? As I recall, your preference is for Extraversion. Mine is for Introversion. All I can tell you is that when someone asks me a question, it's like a marble being dropped into one of those multilevel puzzles with holes in each layer. It starts rolling around, finds the hole and drops to the next layer, finds the hole there and drops through to the next layer, and so forth until it falls out the bottom. When it falls out, I have a response. I am not consciously withholding anything. Nor am I stupid or slow. I simply prefer to process internally before I respond. In fact, if I respond too quickly it may mean I have a prefabricated answer that has been designed to cover some- thing up!" As the truth of this explanation dawned on him, George began to turn very pale. John touched him on the arm and asked what was wrong. George whispered, ashamed, "I can't tell you how many people I've fired because I thought I couldn't trust them."

Consider the converse situation, in which a person with Introverted preference observes an Extravert initiating and moving around in many interactions in a short period of time. The Introvert may view such behavior as shallow and superficial. Keep in mind that an Introvert engaged in this behavior may indeed feel shallow and superficial, and therefore assumes others would feel the same. The Introvert's baseline is all wrong for making sense of the Extravert's behavior.

Missed Associations

Whatever a person's preference, the behavior of a person with the opposite preference seems inconsistent and out of synch with our experience. Never mind that to the second person, the associations the first person is making are all wrong and lead to a complete misjudgment. Given the studies showing that we assess and make up our minds about people within thirty seconds of meeting them, it seems important to keep this kind of cross-preference projection in mind. It is most pronounced between Extraversion and Introversion, but missed associations happen at every level between the individual preferences and among whole types. It is therefore vital to know that the message you intend to send may not be reaching your audience.

With the Extravert's typical hunger for pace, variation, and expressive engagement, it is easy to see how people in committed relationships can get into trouble. The energy they put into engaging in the world may be interpreted by Introverts in their life as leaving little energy for them. Likewise, the Extravert may feel that the energy an Introverted partner puts into internal analysis denies him the important insights needed to solve the problem before them.

It is safe to assume that people engaged in the environment and interacting with others are *expressing* Extraversion. In that mode, their comments may simply be the beginning or middle of thought, not the end. They may be probing for reactions, and if so their comments may have no more significance than to simply spur the conversation. They are constantly misunderstood as meddling, opinionated, and forceful, but if you listen carefully and hold your judgments in tow, you may hear information that reveals the richness of thought and the intent of the message.

When individuals are observant, somewhat disengaged, and seem careful about word choice, it is reasonable to assume they are *expressing* Introversion. In this mode, their comments are usually the end parts of their thoughts. What comes out verbally is their most complete thought on the topic for the time being. Receptive and appearing cautious, they are simply trying to create space in their environment to let their heads work. Typically oblivious to being seen as guarded, their pace may simply allow their minds to be undistracted as they sort through their experiences. But they generally share what is important to them, and if you listen carefully you will get a very good idea of their mind-set and perspective. They are not holding back, necessarily; they are simply sorting through all the internal static to become clear on what to finally say. Often misunderstood as aloof, condescending, and anxious, they are actually creating the time and space needed to respond to the experience they are having.

Communication Effects of Sensing and Intuition

If the differences between Extraversion and Introversion lead to misunderstandings of the value and meaningfulness of shared information, the differences between Sensing and Intuition hit at the heart of trust and honesty. There is no more profound difference in communication than the projections developed by these preferences, because they are at the root of building our understanding of reality.

The Essence of Sensing

Sensing, by its nature, finds the information of the moment clear, concise, and concrete. A person with this preference is likely to have an appreciation for brief statements describing the who, what, where, when, how, why, and relative status of the situation. Studies of military personnel consistently show that a large proportion of them report having a Sensing preference: Order, precision, focus, and immediate action are hallmark qualities.[40] Military forms must be filled out with exact information; they do not ask what you think was going on in the heads of folks involved in an incident. Fidelity to the facts of the present is bedrock Sensing.

Contrasting the Intuitive

Nothing could be further from the attention of Intuition than fidelity to facts. For intuition, a fact only begins to have meaning in context to situations; thus, from the Intuitive perspective, the interpretation of a fact may change as the context shifts, and more often than not focusing on facts creates barriers to new ideas! Those with an Intuitive preference are more inclined to imagine the potential outcomes, extrapolate about events and people's motives, and look for information that confirms the reigning theory (about people, situations, or other things). More important to such folks than facts is whether certain perceived principles were honored.

Imagine a meeting of a business team in which three members have a Sensing preference and two have an Intuitive preference. The discussion could be filled with a considerable amount of conflict if one cluster wants to focus on the realistic, present-oriented, concrete elements of a problem and the other two seek to develop multiple alternatives to solve the problem at some point in the future. The abstraction and theoretical interests of the Intuitive will be evident in the language and the questions used during the discussion. Depending on the critical nature of the situation, the pressures could drive these two groups into heated and difficult conflict as each group believes the other is focusing on the wrong set of issues.

A sense of the pragmatic versus a sense of the possible will always stump interactions between Sensing and Intuitive types until they are cognizant of each other. In fact, each can easily begin to believe the other is idiotic. Sensing types often are baffled at the language used by Intuitives and at their apparent focus on the future, the theoretical, and the abstract. "How can a simple question generate so much stuff?," Sensing types often wonder. "Why can't they see more in this information, see its paradoxical meaning?" say the Intuitives about the Sensing types. Because the influence of perception is the fountainhead to the operation of the psyche, these differences are profound. And the profound nature of these differences can be seen in the speed with which distrust can be created among people of goodwill.

Communication Effects of Thinking and Feeling

If Sensing and Intuiting perception are at the heart of trust in communication, then Thinking and Feeling are critical to the communication of mutual respect. Thinking types often show their interest and enthusiasm by critiquing their experiences and the information put in front of them. Feeling types, by contrast, show their interest and enthusiasm by identifying and expressing appreciation for important aspects of their experiences and the information put before them.

"Stepping Out" for Clarity

Trying to step out of the situation in which they find themselves in order to gain clarity, individuals with a Thinking preference seek to find criteria that can frame information and experience in such a way that there is a sense of objective analysis. It seems objective because of the logical, orderly manner in which situations are reviewed. Folks with a Thinking preference put enormous effort into looking at the pros and cons of a situation, analyzing how things are related, and proposing principles to guide their thoughts.

"Stepping In" for Awareness

Those with a Feeling preference want to step in to a situation and have a very specific awareness of how people in the situation are affected. Feeling types immediately focus on the consequences of contemplated actions or real choices in terms of the people involved. Acutely aware that reasoned criteria are valuable for decisions, those with a Feeling preference have an automatic personal value system that places specific human well-being above any externally imposed system of analysis. Knowing full well the argument that decisions are made in business to ensure the well-being of the greatest number of employees, the Feeling type's concern for the outcomes on individual human beings nevertheless remains undaunted.

There is often the danger, when exploring Thinking and Feeling, of people taking the definitions too far. Thinking types have feelings and values that inform their analysis; Feeling types use reason and logic to assist their judgment. But the primary basis of the judgment they use is profoundly different.

Define Conflict and Give Three Examples

When people grouped together by preference are asked to define conflict and give three examples, they consistently respond in the following general ways.

Thinking types: Conflict exists whenever two or more people disagree for so long that emotions get involved. It is often very productive and useful and enables us to get to the heart of issues and make better decisions. Take, for example, some wars that are very useful, some corporate actions that are critical to competitiveness, and even some vigorous arguments at home that clear the air.

Feeling types: Conflict exists when we disagree. It is often avoided because of the discomfort created. It is rarely useful and gets in the way. A clear example is the conflict evident when people argue or debate.

Can individual realities be so different? Driven by a framework of fair play, those with a Thinking preference are inclined to assume that everyone values that playing field. Focused on a value of avoiding harm to others, those with a Feeling preference naturally assume that anyone choosing to make others uncomfortable simply does not honor other people over their need to be right or correct. Consider this dialogue:

Teacher: I had to fail three students last year in my English class. I've seen those kids since then and I worry about their self-esteem.

Principal: You shouldn't worry about them. They chose not to do the work. We need to be careful not to let our emotions override standards for performance.

Teacher: First of all, I said they failed, so my standards are very much in place. Second, my emotions are not involved with these students, as you're suggesting, but they are getting involved with this discussion.

Principal: I was merely trying to make the point that standards are important.

Teacher: I was merely pondering whether we are attending to the self-esteem of these kids so they will grow up to be caring and productive adults! I don't need to justify my feelings or my standards.

Potential Loss of Respect

The teacher's comments are a fairly typical Feeling reaction, and the principal's are a fairly typical Thinking response. This type of interaction leads to the false conclusion that one does not really respect the other. It would be easy for either one to walk away with the awareness of being misunderstood and perhaps even feeling unappreciated. And as we noted at the beginning of this section, this dimension has the greatest affect on the sense of mutual respect between people during interactions. Often the source of considerable interpersonal pain and discomfort, the language of Thinking and Feeling prompts deeply felt reactions.

If the role of projection is as critical as it seems, the loss of respect between persons with these differences is understandable. Because the Thinking type judgment process relies on logic, it quickly and constructively responds to a logical presentation of information. Thinking types tend to communicate respect to a person whose presentation is elegantly logical, that is, with the conclusion following efficiently from the premise without the static of interpersonal overtones or caveats. We know that a Thinking type is dedicated and even passionate about things when he or she thoroughly critiques them. Thinking types report that they know a person respects them when they receive feedback about what they can do to improve the next presentation or project.

On the other hand, Feeling types have enormous energy associated with the awareness of accepting and being accepted. They tend to communicate respect through acceptance. Often what they most want in an interaction, before continuing a discussion, is an initial indication that the other individual finds them acceptable as persons.

Feeling types say that they know a person respects them when the feedback is initially about the importance of the individual contribution and effort before discussing the range of improvements that could be made in a presentation or project.

Communication Effects
of Judgment and Perception

Isabel Briggs Myers carried Jung's theory of types to its fullest extension by focusing on the dynamic within each type. As discussed earlier, we extravert either judgment or perception and introvert the opposite of what is extraverted. Myers had to struggle with how to get at such subtle distinctions when constructing the MBTI inventory. We developed the following material about her Judging–Perceiving dimension to identify the preferred mental function in the Extraverted mode. For example, Myers' assumption is that an ENFP extraverts Intuition and introverts Feeling. But like the other dimensions at the core of psychological type, this carries with it another layer of interactional issues. With this exploration we begin wading into the dynamics of the types.

Judgment in the Extraverted mode, whether Thinking or Feeling, is an orientation toward observable decision making. The attraction of closure is strong for those who extravert their judgment function. Often desirous of a methodical and systematic approach, those who sort Judgment on the *Myers-Briggs Type Indicator* instrument are indicating that you are likely to see and hear decisive action from them.[41] The message often received by others who run into Extraverted Judgment is one of impatience and bare tolerance of anything that slows down the action.

Decision Now or Later

Those who extravert Perception give the message that they are concerned about the negative consequences of making premature decisions. Preferring to trust data, they find almost any information useful and tend to seek out interactions that move among several different topics before settling on any given one. This often annoys those who are ready to make something happen now by making a decision.

Unfortunately, given the speed with which decisions about other people are made upon first meeting them, this observable behavior can trigger all kinds of preconceptions. Extraverted Perceptive types often see those with Extraverted Judgment as rigid, dogmatic, and pushy; Extraverted Judgers often see those with Extraverted Perception as ineffectual, inefficient laggards. For example, in a committee meeting where a person who extraverts Judgment (ET, EF) wants a time limit for discussion on each topic, often the Extraverted Perceiver (EN, ES) will object that doing so feels confining and could cause the group to lose out on important late-breaking information. When the Extraverted Perceiver wants to keep the discussion going past the agreed upon time, often the Extraverted Judger feels that the other person is wasting time, looking at irrelevant material, and waiting too long to act.

Value of Type Dynamics in Communication

This look at the dimensions of type—Extraversion, Introversion, Sensing, Intuition, Thinking, Feeling, and Myers' Judgment and Perception qualities—leads to the core issue in using type constructively in communication: the dynamics of the types. While the broad necessities of communications—trust, honesty, and respect—are certainly influenced by the expression of the preferences, the more complex and often truer examination of communication is discovered by analyzing the types' dynamics.

To review, each of the sixteen types is a combination of the uses of extraverted and introverted judgment and perception. For easy reference, the constellation of types follows. Keep in mind that the extraverted functions play the most observable initial role in our efforts to communicate with others.

	Lead Function	**Support Function**
ISTJ	Introverted Sensing	Extraverted Thinking
ISFJ	Introverted Sensing	Extraverted Feeling
INFJ	Introverted Intuition	Extraverted Feeling
INTJ	Introverted Intuition	Extraverted Thinking
ISTP	Introverted Thinking	Extraverted Sensing

ISFP	Introverted Feeling	Extraverted Sensing
INFP	Introverted Feeling	Extraverted Intuition
INTP	Introverted Thinking	Extraverted Intuition
ESTP	Extraverted Sensing	Introverted Thinking
ESFP	Extraverted Sensing	Introverted Feeling
ENFP	Extraverted Intuition	Introverted Feeling
ENTP	Extraverted Intuition	Introverted Thinking
ESTJ	Extraverted Thinking	Introverted Sensing
ESFJ	Extraverted Feeling	Introverted Sensing
ENFJ	Extraverted Feeling	Introverted Intuition
ENTJ	Extraverted Thinking	Introverted Intuition

By now you have sorted yourself several times while reading this book, and perhaps have completed the MBTI inventory itself; thus you have some initial hypothesis of your type preferences. As you review the expressions of the types in table 13, consider both your type and the expressions of those with whom you interact every day. For each type dynamic, we outline in table 13 how it is are likely to be expressed in matters of communication. Specifically, we explore the role of the types' dynamics in basic informational projections, preferred relationship qualities, typical emotional buttons, and constructive reframing of communications.

Informational Projections as Influenced by Type

If we want to learn how to listen closely to other people, and in so doing learn the general content of their thought and the intent of their communication, we need to know the way information is generally sorted and saved. For example, if I know you are attracted to information that is testable and verifiable, and that you associate precision in details with clarity of judgment, then it would benefit our interaction for me to strive to express information in those ways. Further, if you tend to express or react in a calm, unassuming manner, the chances are that attempting to wow you with status, credentials, and prestige will not be effective in establishing credibility. Credibility is established through the verifiable and precise data presented in the interaction.

Table 13 reviews the information attractive to, associations made by, and expressions common to each of the sixteen types. These are the bases by which people make projections on the information they get while interacting with others. The information

TABLE 13

TYPE PATTERNS OF INFORMATION PROJECTIONS

ISTJ

Introverted Sensing With Extraverted Thinking

Information attracted to   Tested and verifiable data that are easily analyzed

Associations made   Precision in detail leads to clarity of thought

Expressions offered   Generally presents oneself in an unassuming manner, preferring to express information in a calm, careful way

ISFJ

Introverted Sensing With Extraverted Feeling

Information attracted to   Consistent and reliable data that aid people

Associations made   Steady and realistic information leads to loyalty

Expressions offered   Generally fastidious, careful, preferring to express information about people in an unhurried fashion

INFJ

Introverted Intuition With Extraverted Feeling

Information attracted to   Ideas related to people; idealistic belief in theory

Associations made   Actions reflect motives

Expressions offered   Generally appreciative in comments and, though often appearing somewhat scholarly, is quite inclusive and warm

INTJ

Introverted Intuition With Extraverted Thinking

Information attracted to   Theories supported by analytical thought and systematic evidence examined by a variety of sources

Associations made   Reasonableness and mental versatility lead to real contributions

Expressions offered   Usually observations contain a formula about their experiences; action-oriented comments are quite systematic

TABLE 13 (CONTINUED)

TYPE PATTERNS OF INFORMATION PROJECTIONS

ISTP

Introverted Thinking With Extraverted Sensing

Information attracted to	Present, thorough data that show who, what, when, where, and how
Associations made	Detached analysis focused on practical issues leads to clarity about what should be done when
Expressions offered	Often quiet organizers of data, they ask questions to get specificity about the situation they are in. When talking, they make practical observations

INTP

Introverted Thinking With Extraverted Intuition

Information attracted to	Theories, models, and imaginative connections among ideas
Associations made	Independent skeptical thought will provide a better analysis of a situation
Expressions offered	Initially critical and skeptical in comments; detachedly curious about situations

ISFP

Introverted Feeling With Extraverted Sensing

Information attracted to	Pragmatic information that is related to other people
Associations made	Thorough, reliable information will provide for realistic action
Expressions offered	Warmth and good-natured conversation seem easy; comments are gentle, factual, realistic

INFP

Introverted Feeling With Extraverted Intuition

Information attracted to	Drawn to information that is reflective of values
Associations made	Introspective consideration of circumstances will lead to ideas that promote harmony and innovation
Expressions offered	Often deferent in interactions; comments seem unconventional; identifies and expresses complex ideas

TABLE 13 (CONTINUED)

TYPE PATTERNS OF INFORMATION PROJECTIONS

ESTP

Extraverted Sensing With Introverted Thinking

Information attracted to	Present-oriented practical data that aids action now
Associations made	Reliable and thorough action now will secure a realistic future in relationships and work
Expressions offered	Generally engaging with practical suggestions, though critical and forceful comments may be made

ESFP

Extraverted Sensing With Introverted Feeling

Information attracted to	Data about people and their situations
Associations made	Knowing who, what, where, and when will show care and concern for the well-being of others
Expressions offered	Energetic observations about people and how to aid them in taking the next practical action

ENFP

Extraverted Intuition With Introverted Feeling

Information attracted to	Ideas that promote selected values
Associations made	Active, enthusiastic sharing is resourceful
Expressions offered	Verbally fluent information that is friendly and directed toward harmonious interaction

ENTP

Extraverted Intuition With Introverted Thinking

Information attracted to	Excited about new ideas that are original
Associations made	Uninhibited analysis will lead to resourceful and adaptable choices
Expressions offered	Independent-minded, imaginative, and clever comments; likes to question situations but ultimately looks for a strategy to competently adapt

TABLE 13 (CONTINUED)

TYPE PATTERNS OF INFORMATION PROJECTIONS

ESTJ

Extraverted Thinking With Introverted Sensing

Information attracted to	Verifiable data collected in a systematic way
Associations made	Logical and tested options provide for practical action
Expressions offered	Energetic, analytical observations that are practical and critical show concern for realistic action

ENTJ

Extraverted Thinking With Introverted Intuition

Information attracted to	Analytical information derived from systematic observation
Associations made	Conceptual frameworks that make sense of experience are indicative of a resourceful mind
Expressions offered	Critical about situations and options; often seem impatient to others; value intellectual matters, leading to comments that give formula-like responses

ESFJ

Extraverted Feeling With Introverted Sensing

Information attracted to	Data connecting with people issues and problems
Associations made	Sociable and friendly comments promote cooperation and realistic action
Expressions offered	Often expressive and affiliative in interaction; sympathetic but cooperative action-oriented remarks

ENFJ

Extraverted Feeling With Introverted Intuition

Information attracted to	Ideas and abstractions that help understand people
Associations made	Warm, caring people who are idealistic can make important social contributions
Expressions offered	Expressive and sociable in interactions, but some formality in comments; appreciative of others; often make comments that get at the heart of the issue

individuals find interesting is likely to be part of their outlook and conversations. Associations individuals make about their experience determine a good deal about what they are willing to listen to in conversations and presentations. Finally, how people express themselves is unique to the individual, but there is enough consistency among same-type individuals to free us from instantly judging the intent of their remarks. Table 13 is based on a decade of asking and listening to hundreds of each of the sixteen types.

This information about the way type influences communication gives us an extraordinary opportunity to listen anew to comments made by others. It's a mine-free, efficient pathway to understanding the differences between people that so often lead relationships into trouble. With some patience—a mental counting to ten—we can avoid unnecessary confusion in our efforts to communicate. The hints above give us a way, based on psychological type, to present and hear information without blame or judgment. At the very least we can see that there are so many differences it would behoove us to take the time to ask, "What did you mean by that?" and then really listen to the response.

Preferred Relationship Qualities as Influenced by Type

Assuming that most normal, healthy relationships have trustful, honest, and nonjudgmental aspects to them, it would be valuable to know how the habits of mind that make up type experience these qualities. Such insight makes it easier to communicate in ways that promote mutual understanding.

When we have the experience of being told we are untrustworthy, and there is no basis for this observation, it is a surprise and often disquieting. One of our working assumptions is that normal people like to be seen as trustworthy and that there is bewilderment at being seen otherwise. In a similar fashion, people like to be thought of as honest. Being honest means that your comments do not conceal hidden agendas. Additionally, most people like their comments to be heard as perceptions based on their experience rather than accusations or judgments about others. We may be stunned to learn that a comment intended as a statement of how we see a situation was instead taken personally. Table 14 lists how the types experience these three qualities. It is critical to note that exploring these qualities with people with whom you have relationships can dramatically aid in actually creating these qualities in communication.

The Only Way We Know How

The way we express trust and what we seek out as trusting are essentially the same. Those who trust information that has been consistent over time are likely not to trust so easily those who innovate, where little is consistent over time. The reverse is also true: Those who trust innovation are less likely to feel particularly trusting of those who recite the same facts repeatedly. Gaining clarity about what we easily trust informs us as to what we might *mistake* as untrustworthy.

In a similar vein, we are honest in the only way we know how to be. If you consider honesty to be accurate and precise information, you are less likely to trust people who focus on global impressions. What one person reveals as part of what he or she considers an honest discussion, another may consider inappropriate and raise doubts about the judgment of the person who is trying to communicate.

Finally, the way we act during interactions is rarely ever intended to send a message that is judgmental. We want to be heard for what we mean without being seen as judgmental; thus, when we are direct or sympathetic with the situation of another person, we are telling the "truth" as we see it without blaming.

With these thoughts in mind, consider the descriptions in table 14 for the sixteen types that respond to these questions and statements: "What do they trust?"; "Expresses honesty through . . . or experiences honesty in others who . . . ?"; and finally, "Is being nonjudgmental when offering . . . ." (Note that the lead or dominant preference is listed first, and the support or auxiliary preference is second.)

Most of us wish we experienced more trust, honesty, and nonjudgmental qualities in our relationships. However, in the stress and pace of today's work and home life, we rarely allow ourselves the time to foster and develop these qualities in relationships. But with the "leg up" that type provides, we can get closer to establishing those qualities we most earnestly desire in interactions with others.

Typical Prejudices, Preconceptions, and Emotional Hot Buttons

Along with discomfort about trust, honesty, and judgment, we are vulnerable to other interactional discomforts. Because of the speed of communication today and the demands of the moment, we are

TABLE 14

TYPE PATTERNS IN KEY RELATIONSHIP QUALITIES

ISTJ

Introverted Sensing With Extraverted Thinking

Trust	Information shared over time that is consistent
Honesty	Precision, accuracy, and timeliness
Nonjudgmental	Direct, concise, descriptive comments

ISFJ

Introverted Sensing With Extraverted Feeling

Trust	People who are reliable and who do what they say they will do
Honesty	Show me and tell me and I'll know your honest feelings
Nonjudgmental	Sympathetic expressions of practical hands-on caring

INFJ

Introverted Intuition With Extraverted Feeling

Trust	Values that promote human well-being
Honesty	Recognize the effects of their comments on individuals
Nonjudgmental	Feelings and ideas that are persistently applied

INTJ

Introverted Intuition With Extraverted Thinking

Trust	Analytical frameworks freely offered and based on data
Honesty	Connecting actions, motives, and outcomes in situations
Nonjudgmental	Specific observations about patterns and how these affect systems

TABLE 14 (CONTINUED)

TYPE PATTERNS IN KEY RELATIONSHIP QUALITIES

ISTP

Introverted Thinking With Extraverted Sensing

Trust — Information derived from experience

Honesty — Precise observations about current situations

Nonjudgmental — Candid statement about what is currently happening

INTP

Introverted Thinking With Extraverted Intuition

Trust — Good sound theory supported by analytical observations

Honesty — Find paradox more honest than factual accounts

Nonjudgmental — Critical review of models and information that is validating

ISFP

Introverted Feeling With Extraverted Sensing

Trust — Actions that help people

Honesty — Show intentions in actions, not in words

Nonjudgmental — Lessons on how to care successfully

INFP

Introverted Feeling With Extraverted Intuition

Trust — Personal intuitions about people and situations

Honesty — Reflective summary of thoughts and ideas

Nonjudgmental — Actions that avoid causing harm may result in not sharing data

TABLE 14 (CONTINUED)

TYPE PATTERNS IN KEY RELATIONSHIP QUALITIES

ESTP

Extraverted Sensing With Introverted Thinking

Trust	Precision in the moment; concise interactions
Honesty	Good-natured interactions recognizing the pace of change
Nonjudgmental	Focus on the moment by attending to specifics

ESFP

Extraverted Sensing With Introverted Feeling

Trust	Consistent sharing over time
Honesty	Telling the facts as tempered with concern for others' reactions
Nonjudgmental	Caring for others, enjoying the moment, arousing liking in people

ENFP

Extraverted Intuition With Introverted Feeling

Trust	Enthusiastic engagement related to selective values
Honesty	Sharing the big picture, touching on the human side of the image
Nonjudgmental	Perpetual innovation as a resourceful act

ENTP

Extraverted Intuition With Introverted Thinking

Trust	Competent analysis
Honesty	Acknowledging the complexity of information without simplifying
Nonjudgmental	Critique as part of the analysis needed to adapt

TABLE 14 (CONTINUED)

TYPE PATTERNS IN KEY RELATIONSHIP QUALITIES

ESTJ

Extraverted Thinking With Introverted Sensing

Trust	Tested data presented in a realistic manner
Honesty	Careful but often direct feedback
Nonjudgmental	Critique and analysis as a way to develop loyalty

ENTJ

Extraverted Thinking With Introverted Intuition

Trust	Energetic critical analysis that is theory-based
Honesty	Expressive about perceived motives and theoretical thoroughness
Nonjudgmental	Reasonable and mentally versatile critiquing to achieve results

ESFJ

Extraverted Feeling With Introverted Sensing

Trust	Friendly and inclusive interactions addressing human concerns
Honesty	Unassuming descriptions that support conventions
Nonjudgmental	Exploring ideas through facts as a way to get cooperative action

ENFJ

Extraverted Feeling With Introverted Intuition

Trust	Cooperative interactions that are sympathetic to people
Honesty	Sharing how information and reactions support or discount others
Nonjudgmental	Expressiveness and gregariousness as a way to gain information

unlikely to recognize what's happening when somebody pushes our emotional buttons. Everyone has them; they simply vary depending on personality type. We forget about them until they're pushed, but then they trigger emotions that may be experienced as internal disgust or external agitation. Why do we forget about them? Because human beings are creatures of comfort, and we move away from discomfort as quickly as possible. But knowing what bothers us most gives us an unusual opportunity to recognize misplacement of our energy and to redirect our communications in a way that utilizes our strengths.

Table 15 lists the most common prejudices, preconceptions, and emotional hot buttons of each of the sixteen types, once again based on the responses that people of all types gave to related questions.

Insofar as we are able to get a handle on prejudices, preconceptions, and hot buttons, we have a chance to understand some of the reactions we give to or get from people during conversations. We are all surprised now and then by our own reactions to certain discussion topics, and by the way some of our innocently meant comments seem to bother others. We have an opportunity here to learn to be more forgiving of ourselves and others by understanding that emotional triggers affect everyone; they do so because they impinge, in one way or another, on something we hold dear—perhaps even on one of the reasons we get up in the morning, get to the meeting on time, or keep trying to improve our individual and collective opportunities.

To move beyond simple recognition that our emotional buttons have an orderly basis, and to use the same basis to reframe our experiences, is a step toward constructive communications with others. Gaining knowledge about informational patterns, sources of preferred qualities in communication, and sources of bias in communication gives us insights into the complexity of human interchange. But our exploration of this complexity would be incomplete if we failed to look at how we typically reframe information to aid our understanding. Further, we need to consider the overall style of the sixteen types; this gives us the best impression of their efforts to communicate.

Constructive Reframing of Communications

After years of interactions, most of us are generally aware when our messages are not being received or understood. In response, we

TABLE 15

TYPE PATTERNS IN PREJUDICES, PRECONCEPTIONS, AND HOT BUTTONS

ISTJ

Introverted Sensing With Extraverted Thinking

Prejudices	Impressionistic data are worthless; tell what you see, not what you think
Preconceptions	Competence is related to precision of analysis; concise statements reflect clear thinking
Hot buttons	Challenge either the competency or the factual basis of an analysis

ISFJ

Introverted Sensing With Extraverted Feeling

Prejudices	Theory without practice has little value
Preconceptions	Service to people or institutions has inherent value and virtue
Hot buttons	Debate, argument, or sustained disagreement

INFJ

Introverted Intuition With Extraverted Feeling

Prejudices	Fostering human growth begins with an inner vision
Preconceptions	Details get in the way of working with ideas
Hot buttons	Loss of private space, incomplete issues in interactions

INTJ

Introverted Intuition With Extraverted Thinking

Prejudices	Analytical decisions provide useful information for action
Preconceptions	Introspection promotes theory and encourages thorough analysis
Hot buttons	Loss of autonomy through structure, undervaluing intellectual development

TABLE 15 (CONTINUED)

TYPE PATTERNS IN PREJUDICES, PRECONCEPTIONS, AND HOT BUTTONS

ISTP

Introverted Thinking With Extraverted Sensing

Prejudices	Theory gets in the way of practical action
Preconceptions	Skeptical analysis is reliable and thorough
Hot buttons	Group work that tolerates philosophical discussion and loses sight of tangible goals

INTP

Introverted Thinking With Extraverted Intuition

Prejudices	Thoroughly analyze quietly before you talk; only independent and autonomous people are imaginative
Preconceptions	Somebody else's model is more complete because it is so critical and analytical
Hot buttons	Poor logical arguments; doubts about the integrity of one's own analysis

ISFP

Introverted Feeling With Extraverted Sensing

Prejudices	Noisy people don't reflect very much and therefore cannot be thorough when attending to details
Preconceptions	Knowing the details—who, where, what, when—helps you know and care for people
Hot buttons	Negative feedback, loss of collaboration among people

INFP

Introverted Feeling With Extraverted Intuition

Prejudices	Conventional thinking leads to poor problem solving due to the lack of innovation and flexible resources
Preconceptions	Interpersonal harmony is more valuable than conflict; introspective reflection is more effective than group problem solving
Hot buttons	Assertions of a lack of caring, questioning of motives, being seen as touchy and interpersonally suspicious

TABLE 15 (CONTINUED)

TYPE PATTERNS IN PREJUDICES, PRECONCEPTIONS, AND HOT BUTTONS

ESTP

Extraverted Sensing With Introverted Thinking

Prejudices	Past is dead; future can't be predicted, so focus on now
Preconceptions	Knowing specifics will lead to practical action
Hot buttons	Unrealistic and impractical suggestions

ESFP

Extraverted Sensing With Introverted Feeling

Prejudices	Good-natured people are reliable and thorough
Preconceptions	Being practical makes sense in helping people; having a great deal of energy reflects a person's action orientation
Hot buttons	Unkind critical comments; people who detach from a situation

ENFP

Extraverted Intuition With Introverted Feeling

Prejudices	Closed-minded people; slow and unenthusiastic interactions suggest an unadaptable mind-set
Preconceptions	If they generate lots of ideas, people will not mind implementing them; being friendly and adaptable means you agree
Hot buttons	Questioning beliefs or values, challenging ideas put forth, managing implementation procedures

ENTP

Extraverted Intuition With Introverted Thinking

Prejudices	Being verbally fluent and adaptable means you are resourceful; analysis and intellectual development are best
Preconceptions	Good thinking leads to good action; being adaptable means you will have more opportunities
Hot buttons	Questioning depth and competence; suggesting responsibility for the effects of remarks

TABLE 15 (CONTINUED)

TYPE PATTERNS IN PREJUDICES, PRECONCEPTIONS, AND HOT BUTTONS

ESTJ

Extraverted Thinking With Introverted Sensing

Prejudices	Reasonable and analytical people are more resourceful
Preconceptions	Once the data are verified, act fast for best results; only action-oriented people who are analytical get things done
Hot buttons	Disloyal, unorganized, dreamy people

ENTJ

Extraverted Thinking With Introverted Intuition

Prejudices	Mentally versatile people make real contributions; proactive and systematic decision making leads to the best conclusions
Preconceptions	Action, fast pace, high aspirations, and analytical people are intelligent and more capable than others at getting things done
Hot buttons	Nonteam players, people who are not bright, people who have no critical or analytical conversation

ESFJ

Extraverted Feeling With Introverted Sensing

Prejudices	Friendly and sympathetic people are loyal and inclusive
Preconceptions	Only through strong relationships can you really get things done
Hot buttons	Cool, detached people who are more interested in their own thoughts than in sharing with others

ENFJ

Extraverted Feeling With Introverted Intuition

Prejudices	Warm, responsive people are likely to work cooperatively together
Preconceptions	Being sympathetic and idealistic are the best qualities for working with people
Hot buttons	People who exclude others and who are detached from sharing; withdrawn people who show no appreciation

frequently attempt to rephrase what we said in a way that we hope will clarify it. Most often, though, our rephrasing is simply an enlargement of the original. When, for example, we explain the concept of time to a child by using a broad focus, if the child doesn't understand at first we may shift to an even broader focus. Only after several unsuccessful attempts with that strategy might it occur to us to try a different method entirely—concrete examples, perhaps. Conversely, someone who begins with concrete examples may eventually resort to using broad concepts to get the point across.

Such a new strategy is simply a different cut of prior effort; taking a new angle in this way is called reframing. Whenever you hear yourself with a hint of frustration in your voice, and then begin a new sentence with words such as, "Okay—let me try to explain it another way . . ." you are attempting to reframe the concept or issue at hand. The impulse is good—reframing attempts to find the words that allow all parties to be winners.

In our effort to share information, to be understood, and to make a contribution, we rely on our past experiences. Our general interactive style has been reinforced and encouraged partly due to our biases for certain information. But in the end, our style and our expressions come from the heart of who we are. If we are ever going to be able to move from old modes of interaction to new and more effective ways to communicate, we need to understand that we are the message. Our habits of mind collude with our expressions to make up the core of our interpersonal efforts in communication.

Table 16 gives descriptors of the patterns each type employs to clarify and reframe messages. First is a statement about the type's general style, which sets the context for how that type clarifies and then reframes a message. Then comes a description of the typical clarification effort, followed by a suggested reframing strategy for that type based on the kinds of information they may be inclined to overlook.

Our efforts to reframe experience and to regroup in conversations is reflective of the impulse to understand what is put before us. The tools we have to make sense of our experience are a combination of our natural gifts, our wits at the time, and the lessons we have learned. In communicating, we are likely to rely on what is nearest to who we are, for it is the script we know best. The unconscious competence of our habits of mind is exhibited in most of our conversations. We can become more in tune with these habits by knowing how we listen to ourselves, how we reframe, and how we generally communicate. In gaining such clarity, we have the benefit of learning to listen more acutely to others and what they have to offer.

TABLE 16

TYPE PATTERNS IN CLARIFYING COMMUNICATIONS

ISTJ

Introverted Sensing With Extraverted Thinking

General style	Usually so quiet and reserved it is difficult to know how information personally affects them; share logical, factual perspectives in an unhurried and careful manner
Clarification	Attempt understanding by gathering facts and asking questions
Reframing	May need to identify themes and share personal reactions

ISFJ

Introverted Sensing With Extraverted Feeling

General style	Empathetic with those around, warm and thoughtful about others, careful and studied comments about people and situations which are reliable statements of any current situation
Clarification	Calmly go about doing what they think helpful, rarely assert own needs, often test ideas with facts
Reframing	May need to ask about larger issues than those in the present, share critiques

INTJ

Introverted Intuition With Extraverted Thinking

General style	Often collect theories and ideas, can react to most any situation competently, systematic in gathering information, often seem critical and questioning; drive for independence and autonomy seems cool and detached
Clarification	Want interactions to make sense in the big picture, and so ask tougher and more comprehensive questions
Reframing	May need to share thoughtful personal reactions in seeking to be friendly and to test theories with facts

INFJ

Introverted Intuition With Extraverted Feeling

General style	Appreciative in comments, find that interactions suggest the motives and values of conversants, value information about people for its own sake and therefore seem somewhat scholarly—reserved, idealistic, formal
Clarification	Seek to understand motives and personal frameworks for decisions
Reframing	May need to ask about verifiable facts and realistic choices

TABLE 16 (CONTINUED)

TYPE PATTERNS IN CLARIFYING COMMUNICATIONS

ISTP

Introverted Thinking With Extraverted Sensing

General style	Somewhat detached and independent but good-natured style; often imaginative in responses yet questioning seems unconventional and betrays the organized analysis used to make sense of the world
Clarification	Pursue practical and realistic discussion about action to take today, seem skeptical and unconcerned about personal outcomes
Reframing	May need to show more interest in effects of situations on others and to express inclusion of others in conversations

INTP

Introverted Thinking With Extraverted Intuition

General style	Can be very satisfied as detached onlookers asking only questions sufficient to address gaps in the logic of those engaged in discussions; appear adaptable but skeptical and critical
Clarification	Ask more questions, analyze more circumstances, and organize more ideas
Reframing	May need to show more inclusion of and interest in others

ISFP

Introverted Feeling With Extraverted Sensing

General style	Often so introspective that actions of care and concern speak more than words; share practical and reliable information
Clarification	Show interest and concern by becoming more deferent; want to understand by knowing the specifics
Reframing	May need to consider the overall framework and be critical questioners of situations

INFP

Introverted Feeling With Extraverted Intuition

General style	Introspective and gentle; often say whatever will harmonize the conversation or situation; appear adaptable
Clarification	Pursue wider frames of meaning, connecting the conversation to larger contexts
Reframing	May need to look at the facts and attend to the current circumstance regardless of its personal meaning

TABLE 16 (CONTINUED)

TYPE PATTERNS IN CLARIFYING COMMUNICATIONS

ESTP

Extraverted Sensing With Introverted Thinking

General style   Action orientation captured in excitable and energetic attention to the who, what, where, and when of a situation; critical nature overshadowed by ability to ease tensions in the present

Clarification   Focus on the action now and forcefully get at the facts

Reframing   May need to show empathy and ask about personal values

ESFP

Extraverted Sensing With Introverted Feeling

General style   Active practical and realistic response to situations likely to reflect enjoyment of other people; creative at finding hands-on solutions; arouse liking and acceptance

Clarification   Focus on the here-and-now aspects of situations; express and show concern for others

Reframing   May need to be more questioning of the motives and contexts of interactions

ENTP

Extraverted Intuition With Introverted Thinking

General style   Energetically engage in conversation, asking imaginative questions; generally resist conventional actions, prefer original, almost irreverent response; seem adaptable but in fact go along for the ride to collect more information for analysis

Clarification   Ask more skeptical questions and provide more statements of reasonable, logical options

Reframing   May need to step back and observe others, make personal connections before theorizing

ENFP

Extraverted Intuition With Introverted Feeling

General style   Communicate enthusiasm and energy, seem adaptable and open to possibilities, seem to work in spurts but in fact introspect on connection of current situation to similar previous circumstances, friendly and verbally fluent about values

Clarification   Seek more possibilities and more ideas to address a situation

Reframing   May need to focus on one option, collecting sufficient facts to test the strength of an idea

TABLE 16 (CONTINUED)

TYPE PATTERNS IN CLARIFYING COMMUNICATIONS

ESTJ

Extraverted Thinking With Introverted Sensing

General style High energy, hard hitting interactions where practical and realistic action endorsed; fluent about loyalties; may appear so convinced of a formula for making things make sense that they have no patience for other views

Clarification More facts and more logical analysis

Reframing May need to ask more about values and themes, and seek to be more empathetic

ENTJ

Extraverted Thinking With Introverted Intuition

General style Expressive and fluent about analysis, seek to show resourcefulness for helping address a situation; like a fast-paced interaction that provides theory, analysis, action

Clarification Seek understanding by being more critical, more analytical, and more systematic

Reframing May need to show appreciation and express more concern for people involved in a given interaction

ESFJ

Extraverted Feeling With Introverted Sensing

General style Warm and outgoing, loyal and unassuming conversationalists, often inclusive of others; test ideas with facts; careful about actions to ensure no one will be left out; often thorough about facts and fastidious about actions

Clarification Express more empathy and inclusion to gain cooperation

Reframing May need to express more ideas and be more critical about the logic of others' analyses

ENFJ

Extraverted Feeling With Introverted Intuition

General style Engaging socially, outgoing and gregarious, often show appreciation and sympathetic understanding, like ideas and enjoy interactions that add knowledge to personal libraries of possibilities to explore

Clarification Express more personal meaning and seek out more personal information during interactions

Reframing May need to verify facts and test ideas

Engaging the Expressions

To understand others is first to understand ourselves. Being aware of and acknowledging our individual psychology—habits of perception and judgment, including type, personal history, lessons learned, and responses—is first on the list of ways that lead toward communicating well. When we are clear about the typical responses we give, we can then focus more clearly on the expressions others provide. Paradoxical as it might seem, we may become better at listening to others if we know most about our own patterns of communication.

The reason is that if we come to expect certain patterns, we need not project unnecessary (even incorrect) meaning onto other people's comments. For example, knowing that an Extraverted Thinker provides criticism as a basic way to communicate means that one needn't presume that the critique signifies lack of respect. Understanding type means being able to hear people's expressions without unwarranted blame or judgment.

When we stop assuming that what we hear or see is something we necessarily know, we have a clean slate that enables us to ask other people what they really mean if we suspect we missed their true meaning the first time around. Remember the story at the beginning of this chapter? Roger had to ask Olivia what she meant twice before he discerned her needs. So it is with everyone: Asking and listening generates more effective communication.

Of course, sometimes new learning does not simplify our lives at the outset. Psychological type informs us that interactions are rarely simple, and therefore our efforts to improve communications will likely fail if we look only at male-female socialization, or cultural differences, or historical developments. To move forward, we must recognize the full complexity of the individual.

VALUING DIFFERENCES

7

Making Diversity Work

A corporate vice president of operations, age fifty-three, was discussing the promotion of several staff members with the company president when he said about one candidate, "I really can't figure out how his mind works. He's a good producer but he's unconventional and has a really different perspective. I'm not sure we can risk moving him to the new position."

As the chains and belts beat the legs and back of a boy who happened upon a group of teenagers beneath the stands at a high school football game, he cried out, "Why are you doing this to me?" They screamed back, "Because you're different from us."

Perhaps the major psychological problem of our time is that of developing the capacity to value human differences. It seems that no matter where we look, people are in conflict, even at war, because their beliefs are different, their roots are different, or their history is different. Such conflict is inevitable when the underlying assumption of either party is that being different means one side is better, the other worse; one valued, the other worthless; one more important, the other secondary at best. At its extreme, such belief leads to the conclusion that those who are different have no rights—not even the right to live. Even in democracies where difference is supposed to be tolerated, we find enormous rifts among groups of people due to perceived differences and the antagonistic interpretations of those differences.

Some differences are far more obvious and painful than others, but at the root of our response to all of them are individual psychological differences. Even observable differences such as race or physical handicap wouldn't separate people unnecessarily if not for the psychology of the observer. Individuals who believe that other races are inferior or untrustworthy, or who believe they have nothing in common with handicapped people, often simply avoid interacting with them. These beliefs, attitudes, and expectations about others are all part of our individual perspectives, and they aid our management of daily interactions.

Troubling Differences

Certainly some differences are troubling. Individuals who hear voices from God giving them permission to break the law, or people who feel compelled for whatever reason to destroy others, are different in ways that civilized society has declared intolerable. Such differences in behavior and ideas are clearly recognized as unacceptable. Imagine a tolerance continuum: The low end, zero tolerance, is occupied by people who commit heinous crimes because they have no tolerance for difference; the high end is populated by those with absolute openness to other points of view—so confident and comfortable are they with their own values that they feel no threat whatsoever and thus remain completely open to others. Between the two extremes, we would hope that among normal people who work to improve their lives, raise their families, and contribute to the general welfare, there is a long distance between us and zero tolerance. It would be nice if there were only a few differences that each of us found unacceptable. But this is rarely the case. Human behavior seems to be such that once we have declared some differences unacceptable, we extend that reaction to most other differences.

The differences we immediately see are gender and race. Sometimes clothes pinpoint differences in social status. These differences have their own place in the history of human struggle which is beyond the scope of this book. But the differences represented in personality, though more subtle, are subject to the same forces as those in gender, race, or religion. For example, in organizations where we have collected MBTI inventory data on the executives, managers, associates, and newly selected supervisors of the same company, we find that the executives select managers and supervisors who are like themselves, having developed intolerance of those who think differently.[42]

Preferred Flocks

Any way you look at it, we usually like people who are like ourselves. We are more comfortable with them and more accepting of their foibles. The tendency to clan together with those who share interests, world views, political attitudes, and general outlooks on life is basic. It is rooted in the need to socialize with those who support and affirm our needs and experiences. A great deal is being asked of us when we stretch psychologically to embrace difference at any level. So at the outset, we are somewhat programmed to avoid prolonged dealings with those who are really different. This is the first problem in addressing the topic of valuing differences.

A second problem is the equating of understanding with valuing. It is a drastic mistake in logic to conclude that if you are understood, then you are also valued. Understanding that women earn seventy cents while a man doing the same job makes a dollar does not change the fact, nor does it mean that women are valued in any sense more than they are paid. Children often make the mistake of assuming that a parent's understanding of a behavior means permission has been granted to do it. Quickly, however, kids learn that parental understanding of what, when, why, and how does not necessarily mean acceptance of the proposed activity. Understanding is not valuing; understanding is a process in its own right, though it is often a critical step in the valuing process.

Understand Me

There is a national "understand me" craze evident in the numerous diversity training programs throughout industry and government. It is sadly ironic that so many people spend long hours in workshops listening to the stories of others but come away valuing others no more and behaving the same, even if they have achieved an understanding of how others feel and think. Understanding the plight of minorities of our society has done little to change social attitudes toward valuing the contribution they could make to overall society. Seeking to understand is valuable in its own right; the error is in believing that it necessitates valuing others who are different.

We will go so far as to say that those who settle for understanding and being understood have less than fully developed their communication potential. Jung suggested that the notion of being understood really means to be embraced, to be interpreted correctly. Those who have a passion to be understood are merely seeking satisfaction for the most basic impulses—to be embraced and comforted. The only person who really comes close to understanding us in this sense is, in most cases, our mother. So we might consider that to seek only to be understood is to seek the embrace of Mother.[43] While that embrace is temporarily satisfying, it fails the test of maturity. It fails to acknowledge the critical task of a mature human being, which is to develop interdependencies with those who neither understand us nor wish to support us in our quests. Learning to value difference and to act it out may be one of the developmental tasks of adulthood that lead to wisdom.

A Language for Valuing

If liking those who are like ourselves and wanting simply to be understood makes getting at the central nature of valuing difficult, then consider a third issue: We do not have an easy language for valuing. Many of our ideas about valuing are like those of children who think that being understood and valued means getting your way. Clearly, being valued for your difference does not imply that being different guarantees getting your way. Valuing is awkward to describe and analyze. It is difficult to get our minds around the importance of valuing. Like equatorial natives who have no word for snow, maybe we have so few experiences of being valued that our language fails us. We propose that valuing begins with learning about differences and then acting in such ways that those who are different can experience being valued.

The language difficulty is obvious, for example, on the World Wide Web. Surf it sometime and try to find material on valuing. You will find no such discussions or items except about financial matters—evaluation of companies or properties people wish to sell. But on any number of topics such as communication or values, there are hundreds of entries. Read some of them and you will find people are struggling with valuing differences.

Psychological Type Extends Beyond Understanding

Psychological type provides a model to understand and value difference. Type presumes that all preferences for mental processes, for taking in energy, perceiving information, and making decisions are present in the normally functioning individual. These functions enable us to adapt and respond to our daily challenges with more ease and effectiveness. Thus a difference in response is really a matter of appropriateness, not rightness.

Type is a rational way to understand the differences in the ways people respond to events. With the expressions inherent in extraverted or introverted perception and judgment, we have observable differences in behavior. Once we understand the source and nature of these differences, we can reject the notion that they are a threat to our way of seeing the world. As we have seen throughout this book, psychological type provides insights into the way our minds work and the way we respond as a result of these mental habits. Furthermore, type preferences provide a pathway to valuing differences.

Given the Difference, So What?

Why tolerate differences? Why go through the trouble of understanding and then trying to develop behaviors that express a valuing of others? Why is it worth the effort? The answer to all these questions is that personality differences are of major importance to relationships, interactions, decision making, and human development, which certainly makes studying them worthwhile.

The hard truth is that valuing means determining a degree of importance, a measure of worth on some thing, contribution, or experience. We are curious about how to measure the worth of something, and a valuing process is what we use. But curiosity is hardly sufficient to push us toward behaviors of valuing.

The most important reason for us to move toward a perspective of valuing is that the interdependent nature of life means our ability to survive and adapt is directly tied to our ability to manage differences. This is true in one-to-one relationships as well as on a global level.

An Old, Wise Story

Who Speaks for Wolf [44] is a Native American story that provides a compelling case for working toward a way to value differences. As the story goes, a tribe decided to move its village. According to the traditions of the tribe, young men learned to communicate with nature, and when a decision was to be made, they were sent into the wild to learn the lessons of nature. When they returned to share their insights, the tribe gathered to decide, using all the different sources of information.

In this situation, the tribe had sent the young men out to learn what nature would recommend about the tribe's move. All of the young men returned except the one who spoke for the wolf. The tribe chose not to wait for him and acted on the information they had. The decision was a disaster, leading to death and disease. When the wolf boy finally showed up, he told them he knew they should not have moved to that particular place. So the tribe gathered again to consider what to do:

> And so it was that the people devised among themselves a way of asking each other questions whenever a decision was to be made on a New Place or a New Way. [They] sought to perceive the flow of energy through each new possibility and how much was enough, and how much was too much, until at last someone would rise and ask the old question, to remind us of things we do not yet see clearly enough to remember: Tell me my brothers, tell me now my sisters, Who Speaks for Wolf?

> Now among a wise people they will ask what else might be true for them that they did not yet see. They wonder how all these things—seen and unseen—might affect [their] lives and the lives of [their] children's children's children. Then to remind us of the great difficulties that might arise from a single omission of something we forgot to consider, they will ask the ancient question, Tell me my brothers, tell me now my sisters, Who Speaks for Wolf?[45]

As this ancient story informs us, more efficacious decisions are likely to be made, if when valuing the different views, all views are considered. For example, in hundreds of training simulations, groups of people read about a situation and rate actions to take. After individuals rate the actions, the group discusses why each person rated actions in a certain way. If the group allows all views to be aired and discussed freely, the group ratings are usually vastly superior to the individual ratings; in groups where no discussion or debate is tolerated, many individual scores are higher than the group score and the group score is usually lower on average than those of groups who tolerated different views. This outcome illustrates the same point as the Native American story: difference can enrich the lives of all those who promote an environment where differences exist and are valued.

Valuing Means . . .

Valuing means considering each perspective to be important in its own right and providing, through interactions, room for the expression of each perspective without disparagement. While any given perspective may play only a small part in a final decision or conclusion, there still must be room for it to be expressed. Valuing should not mean blind acceptance of another's view, but it does imply passion about the right of the other's view to be heard. Valuing is to behave toward others in such a way that they feel respect. It is an interactional process that opens individuals to creative outcomes while avoiding premature conclusion.

So we begin our consideration of valuing by proposing that goodwill among individuals is a prerequisite; in its absence, no tolerance—much less the valuing of others—is possible. If present, goodwill leads to a motive for learning how to value differences.

Valuing Stages

Consider the following stages when thinking about valuing differences. Each is important and leads to the next. Interestingly, this process will help you no matter what difference is under consideration—culture, race, or psychological mind-set.

STAGE 1 **Preconditions of Valuing**

Approach the interaction with an assumption of goodwill and a belief that through interaction, a synergy will occur to provide a better answer or improved condition than one alone could produce. Commit to sharing observations and thoughts without fear of negative evaluation, but with the expectation of critical consideration.

STAGE 2 **Setting Ground Rules**

Set ground rules to get clarity about the amount of time for the interaction and the intention of the discussion; make explicit the general topics of the discussion or conversation.

STAGE 3 **Interchange**

Spend twice as much time listening as speaking, keeping in mind that each person's perspective comes from his or her experience and personality, which are likely different from your own; constantly seek clarity by asking, paraphrasing, and questioning what you have heard and understood; check your own biases (see chapter 6 on communication) and emotional hot buttons; share thoughts and ideas in a manner consistent with your perspective, and respect the other person's style.

STAGE 4 **Closure**

Summarize understanding and use your knowledge of type preferences as a checklist: got the facts (Sensing), considered the possibilities (Intuition), reviewed the pros and cons (Thinking), initiated action consistent with values (Feeling), made a plan for next discussion (Judgment), and left the door open for new information and how it will be conveyed (Perception).

These stages are a kind of orderly way to communicate valuing. Beginning with an attitude of goodwill and a perspective that differences may lead to enhanced opportunities increases the chance that valuing will occur. Ground rules create a fair playing field for the interaction. Consider how differently you feel when your boss calls to set up a meeting and tells you what the meeting is about rather than simply telling you to show up. Think how differently an interaction could develop if your significant other said, "I need an hour with you to discuss buying a car" versus pulling up in the driveway in a new car and yelling "Surprise!"

Critical Interchange

Listening and talking in a way that allows us to recognize differences in style and perspective while focusing on the intent and content of the communication are keys to valuing. Keep in mind that valuing is what we experience in an interaction, not just what we say or what is said to us. The experience of valuing is tied to all of these stages and is expressed in the way we communicate with each other.

In the previous chapter we discussed the dimensions of communication and how psychological type is part of this effort. We looked at how types create their own biases, express their various styles, and strive to make sense of the content of messages. These issues become more vital when considering how to create an experience of valuing. Communication is the medium that allows the possibility of valuing to occur.

We will approach the types first by understanding the general valuing needed and expressed by the individual preferences. For each of the sixteen types, we will examine the role type dynamics plays in valuing differences.

Valuing Preferences

Like an eagle circling above the forest, we need the broad view of valuing expressed by the preferences before we move to the specific trees—the specific psychological types. Given the importance of each preference to the overall functioning of each individual, it makes sense to explore valuing first by preference and then by the dynamics of the types.

As noted earlier, Extraversion and Introversion are processes by which we initiate and reflect, engage and stand back, or attend to experience outside our skin and inside our skin. As this mental wiring is like electrical wiring, Extraversion and Introversion are the charging poles of our completed circuitry. And while both are essential to normal human functioning, we seem to get our batteries charged primarily through one or the other. Those with an Extraverted preference are energized by their environment; those with an Introverted preference, by what they hold inside for consideration. This dimension is so basic to the personality of the individual that the experience of valuing begins with it.

Valuing With
and Through Extraversion

Extraversion wants external space for events to occur. Expansive in the outer world, Extraversion relishes an opportunity to be expressed. Many Extraverts say that thoughts are not real until they are expressed. So as an elementary aspect of valuing, Extraversion requires action, movement, and experience that can be seen or heard.

Consider the child who is constantly engaged with her environment. She talks about things, manipulates things, and tells you about it while she does it, thoroughly engaged in a somewhat public way with the world around her. If her preference is for

Extraversion and these actions seem to motivate and excite her, she is unlikely to feel valued when her preferred behavior results in regularly being told to shut up, sit quietly, and be a big girl. As she becomes a woman, her desire to initiate, share ideas, and engage may be contained because of that childhood message that her natural expression was unwelcome. This is regrettable on two sides: Other people may never know the richness of her ideas and enthusiasms, and she does not experience the rewards of fully engaging with her environment. By contrast, had she been given a childhood where Extraversion was nurtured, she might have grown up to be expressive and active during interactions, and quite comfortable talking about her ideas and seeking out new experiences.

But to be valued, Extraversion needs an opportunity to play itself out and to receive some feedback about its performance. Feedback, by definition, means a return of energy to its source; there is no judgment about it. To get this opportunity when interacting with others, those with an Extraverted preference should be clear that they need the chance to be heard. Further, they want to be engaged through the interaction because where they start is not likely to be where they will end in the conversation. In general, Extraversion wants the interaction to make ideas more real and to develop them into more complete thoughts. For the Extraverted person, true valuing exists through interaction that encourages the development of thought.

Valuing With
and Through Introversion

Introversion is a process of reflection and reception. When time is provided for the process to occur without interruption, then a value of this process has been expressed. The need for inner space time is vital for Introversion, and the amount of time needed varies by situation. Unlike Extraversion where action leads to clarity, with Introversion stillness leads to clarity and focus.

For Introverts, a question or comment may trigger a reaction which then appears to be withheld. As in an old pinball game, a ball has been released and is moving around and around until it finds the right slot for a score. Introverts are often not withholding; they are waiting for the ball to find the slot before they react. This quality often plays out as a difference in pace in an interaction. While Extraverts demonstrate a fast pace, Introverts may appear not to keep up. But the appearance is deceiving. Consider the question of pace in a different arena: Introverts often prefer reading and other visual stimuli over auditory stimuli when learning or developing an understanding. Average reading speed is about 420 words per minute; average speaking speed is 75 to 100 words per minute. So while Extraversion may look fast and action-oriented, Introversion can actually process more complex information in a much shorter period of time. We all do both and we all need both.

Besides the time and opportunity to reflect, Introversion usually relies on an economy of words. Whereas Extraversion by its nature uses many words and expressions, Introversion tends to rely on as few words as possible to get the point across; language is often carefully and selectively used. This is not to imply that every utterance is the outcome of deep thought; usually, it means that the Introvert so highly values conciseness that it is wired into the process.

To express a valuing of Introversion, time for thought, allowances for pace, and attention to the language used are essential. A few moments may make all the difference in the quality of what is shared as well as the openness with which it is offered. Asking about the ideas shared is likely to lead to a broader understanding of the thought processes involved in reaching a particular conclusion. Likewise, finding the balance between asking for more and bombarding the Introvert with information is an important part of the experience of valuing this function.

Valuing Information
From the Sensing Function

To understand Sensing, the perceptive process that pays attention to the fullness of the moment, one begins with the awareness of physical realities and ends in attention to the present. By design, Sensing is the process that gives us the facts of life. Rooms are not simply painted but are a particular color. Carpets are not merely soft; they have color and design about which we can be specific. Such attention to information that is immediate and present is the nature of Sensing.

This inclination to fully attend to the present often expresses itself in behaviors that are specific, practical, and concrete. For example, if those with a preference for Sensing see a way to solve a problem, they often simply go and do it rather than discuss various options. Information that explains and describes is highly valued. To the Sensing function, an experience is what it is without interpretation: A movie is scenes, costumes, sequencing of action, dialogue, and music—not the epic struggle of good and evil that Intuition, by contrast, may report it to be.

Sensing is pulled to a positive-focused awareness of events in the moment. What happens in the future is speculation that merits little attention from the person with a Sensing preference, unless it can be discussed in realistic terms and is based on projections from current factual information. Grounded in the present, Sensing catalogs information as it is experienced. For this reason, there is often an identification with the familiar and with things that have happened. This results in an appreciation of traditional rituals and acknowledged routes to a given outcome. Given a choice between having an agenda or simply brainstorming at a meeting, Sensing is drawn to the agenda because it will frame the experience and provide nails on which to hang facts.

We value Sensing when we show and express recognition of the facts of a situation and of the practical actions that could be taken. Being sure not to discount factual information and requests for practical direct experience are ways to value Sensing. To value it in each person, we need to celebrate the present and show appreciation for the efficiency of attending to specific information.

Conscientiousness—following through, doing exactly what you said you would do when you said you would do it—is a way of valuing Sensing. Often simple acts of attention—notes, cards, illustrations, phone calls—provide sufficient recognition of the importance of focusing on the present. The challenge is to recognize the matter-of-fact and orderly awareness of the present while encouraging independence and appreciation for the metaphorical processes of Intuition.

Valuing Information
From the Intuiting Function

To those with a Sensing preference, the mere suggestion that an idea or a possibility could be treated as real information borders on the bizarre. How can something that is not verifiable or concrete be perceived as information? Yet this is precisely what Intuition is designed to do: take details that quickly fade to the background and bring to the foreground their patterns, possibilities, and trends.

This tendency pulls on the figurative, the associational, the conceptual nature of an experience, situation, or circumstance. While to the Sensing function a glass has specific qualities and dimensions, to the Intuitive process it is a multiplicity of things—

holder of fluid, potential weapon, piece of art. While the Intuitive is pondering the glass as a metaphor, the Sensing type is focusing on its physical properties and practical uses.

Inherent in this immediate move from current factual information to possibilities is a perceptual autonomy. The Sensing function does not desire autonomy from the practical, concrete facts, but the Intuition function insists on independence, on freedom from the worldly, material present. This independence is often marked by an inventive and unconventional way of doing things.

It is as if the Intuitive tuner uses the antennae of perception to find the patterns in signals rather than a particular signal or frequency. Often theoretical with considerable verbal fluency, those with an Intuitive preference appear appreciative of the complex and abstract. This attraction usually results in very tolerant attitudes, since most things seem quite gray rather than precisely black or white.

Often valued because it produces clever ideas, Intuition is the source of brainstorming. But in environments where standard operating procedures rule the day and innovation is an unrecognized resource, Intuitives soon wither or leave. To value Intuitive processes, we need to invite philosophical and theoretical discussion and to tolerate idiosyncratic conversation that appears to be leading nowhere but may actually be the shortest path to a distant point.

From the outset, a degree of faith is expected from those who value Intuition. Unlike Sensing, where information can be shown to be true or false, Intuition requires us to make a leap from point A to point D; maybe later we will get to B and C. Valuing Intuition means embracing thoughts of what could be while identifying the facts.

Valuing Decisions From Thinking

Thought of as the executive function because of its tendency to establish criteria, evaluate by pros and cons, and select a choice based on logic, the Thinking process seeks decision. Often demanding proof of an assertion, those with a Thinking preference rely on reasoned analysis to produce the best solution.

This process responds to competence verifiable by logical demonstration. For example, those who prefer Thinking often report that acknowledging their competency in addressing a problem is more important than recognizing their effort to contribute. So important is this to the Thinking function that a well-thought-out criticism that leads to improvement in performance is highly valued.

The Thinking function is the mind's way of seeking an impartial standard by which to judge experience. Hopelessly subjective, both the Thinking and the Feeling processes rely on personal, internal abilities; the Thinking function in each of us is the voice seeking orderly, reasonable, logical sense of our experience. Those with Thinking as a preference value endurance, achievement, autonomy, and a vigorous mental approach to problem solving.

One way to value this function is to create an interaction that promotes the independence needed to aggressively pursue answers to questions. Allowing the critique of experience and thought is to provide room for the Thinking function to naturally express itself. When someone seems critical, questioning, and analytical, it may help those around him or her to recognize that from the Thinking perspective these are ways to express a valuing of the experience or object being critiqued. When Thinking types don't value a thing, they don't waste their precious time and talent trying to make it better. Only when they no longer care does the analysis stop.

This is often a difficult part of interacting with those whose preference is for Thinking: Their critique often pushes people away though their intent is to cement a commitment to solving problems. It does no good to argue that your feelings are hurt in an interaction where the focus is on action that was taken. When the Thinking function is engaged, personal emotions are annoying distractions from the pursuit of logical choices. So to honor Thinking, focus on the problem. Make any request to discuss how the decision is being made and its effect on you at a later date. The simple desire of the Thinking function is to have an elegant and efficient analysis. Like well-made crystal; which is clear, bright, and pure, the Thinking process seeks answers that are clear, precise, and complete.

Valuing Decisions From Feeling

Because the word feeling is used in so many contexts, this decision-making function is difficult to explain. We use the word to describe emotion, physical sensation, and opinion: We feel love, we feel velvet and find it soft, we feel that one option is better than another. All these meanings are shadows of the Judgment function.

The Feeling function of decision making is grounded in human connections. At its root are values for well-being and avoidance of harm. This may show up in nurturing behavior, affiliative behavior, or idealistic commitment to a vision of human welfare.

Unlike the Thinking function, which often can be mapped as a sequential, orderly analysis almost anyone can follow, the Feeling function is charted more like a fractal in chaos theory. The Feeling function assumes that there are answers in the patterns of relationships. As in chaos theory, in which strange attractors pull and push on molecules to create patterns, the Feeling function pushes and pulls information to find the pattern as it affects human beings. This force begins with an affirmation of existence and builds the values and patterns around it like the layers of nacre an oyster secretes to create a pearl.

This affirmation expresses itself in a tender, accepting, and accommodating network of behaviors. Often expressing appreciation for the contribution of others, for the creator of an object, or of a situation, those who prefer Feeling behave as if the importance of a contribution is self-evident. It is the part of a presumption that both sides can win in a situation regardless of the problem. The Feeling function carries on a private wager: that trusting your reactions, connections to values, and patterns of relationships will produce a superior result.

These pearls of judgment have no sequential logic; rather, they want to be seen for their inherent value before being analyzed for the price and measure of quality that may be imposed. So to value the Feeling function, we should recognize the contribution, note the expression of commitment, identify the value of the relationship, and invite an empathetic assessment of the situation, problem, or issue.

Often perceiving a loss of respect from others who value critical analysis, those with a preference for the Feeling function find little to affirm their decision making. Told to make a logical argument, they are often forced to ignore what they consider most important in order to find a logical pathway to express their views. But we value this function in conversation when we focus on the values, human relationships, and larger human outcomes on individuals. We can give it equal value in decision making by providing time for those preferring the Feeling function to articulate their view of how a situation will affect the quality of life.

Valuing Orientations for Moving Through the Day: Judgment and Perception

We have noted throughout this book that Myers developed a new dimension in psychological type that helps identify the use of the mental functions in the extraverted and introverted attitudes. These orientations are called judgment and perception: The first pushes toward decision, the other toward new information.

Because of the general nature of this habit of mind, Myers was able to describe those who prefer Judgment in the outer world as desiring closure, structure, and order, and those who prefer Perception in the outer world as seeking spontaneity and more information.

These qualities are generally obvious when dealing with another person. They are noticeable almost immediately, and because of that they are often the first factors used in valuing another's work style, interpersonal reactions, and management of the environment.

Decisive, orderly individuals feel valued when they know there will be a beginning, middle, and end to a discussion. They want a plan of action, or at least a plan to make a plan. Valuing Judgment means saying a kind of interpersonal "yes" to the notion of reaching an eventual conclusion.

But go-with-the-flow individuals often plunge ahead without promise of immediate closure, preferring the unexpected and relishing change. They want to know that decisions can be revisited and reopened. They seek comfort in knowing that people will be flexible in decisions. Often operating *ad hoc*, adding new information as it comes along, individuals with the Perceptive preference feel valued when time is provided to simply wander around, both intellectually and physically.

Dimensions of Valuing
for Each of the Sixteen Types

The view of individual preferences above is a first pass at the ways and means of valuing from a psychological type perspective. But though preferences provide clues, they do not give the complex picture obtainable by considering the dynamics of the types; the complete picture should help us find the ways to better express the valuing of others so urgently needed in human relationships.

As noted over and over in this book, people most often give to others what they themselves most want; we assume that what makes sense to us is best for all, and don't think about what others may actually appreciate more. When we want people to feel our respect and know that we value them, we typically behave toward them as we wish they would behave toward us. But each type has certain conditions under which they feel valued; each type expresses valuing in discrete ways. To value other types, we must learn these ways and grow in whichever of our personal dimensions need attention. If type leads us only to recognize our own traits and to identify how we differ from others, without pulling us into new arenas of growth, then the model serves merely a self-centered need. At a deeper level, however, understanding type can help us genuinely value others, and this is the condition necessary to create community, whether in a single interaction or over many years.

Table 17 takes note of three important factors about valuing: how each of the sixteen types experiences being valued, how each expresses valuing toward other types, and what lesson each needs to learn in order to value others according to the biblical Golden Rule—that is, do unto others as you would have them do unto you.

To genuinely value human differences so that everyone benefits, we need to first recognize that differences are a matter of fact. Differences simply exist; it is nature's way. The next task is to tolerate differences. Finally, with maturity, we must learn to approach differences not just with tolerance, but with goodwill.

To reach such a state of maturity, it helps to understand that the sources of these differences are basic human patterns of Perception and Judgment. Once the pattern is recognized and the ensuing behavioral expressions understood, we have an opportunity to follow a process of valuing that leads to mutual respect and reciprocal contributions to human well-being.

Psychological type gives us a pathway to explore human differences. Type theory assumes that all of the mental operations—Extraversion, Introversion, Sensing, Intuiting, Thinking, and Feeling—are of equal value, and that they each play an equal role in our ability to adapt and adjust to our daily challenges. Think of it as a theory of mental equity. More importantly, the management of differences is first and foremost a matter of individual psychology, and psychological type gains us some access to the way our minds work.

Isabel Briggs Myers wrote, "It is not too much to hope that wider and deeper understanding of the gifts of diversity may eventually reduce the misuse and non-use of those gifts. It should lessen the waste of potential, the loss of opportunity, and the number of dropouts and delinquents. It may even help with the prevention of mental illness. Whatever the circumstances of your life, whatever your personal ties, work, and responsibilities, the understanding of type can make your perceptions clearer, your judgments sounder, and your life closer to your heart's desire."[46]

Recognizing those gifts, acknowledging their role and natural expressions, and making a place for them in your conversations and relationships promise to provide a bridge between differences and invite a celebration of the value in human diversity.

TABLE 17

TYPE PATTERNS IN APPLYING THE "GOLDEN RULE"

ISTJ

Introverted Sensing With Extraverted Thinking

Experiences valuing when	Order, structure, and logical analysis are evident
Expresses valuing by	Organizing, detailing, and analyzing a situation
Most needs to learn that	Those who are questioning and value-oriented are providing a structure and analysis worth attention

ISFJ

Introverted Sensing With Extraverted Feeling

Experiences valuing when	Careful, observant attention to others is evident
Expresses valuing by	Showing thoughtfulness with bringing order and making sure people are comfortable
Most needs to learn that	Those who are analytical and open-ended are showing a kind of caring

INFJ

Introverted Intuition With Extraverted Feeling

Experiences valuing when	Ideas for helping others are given validity in discussion, and plans are made to implement ideas
Expresses valuing by	Acting on information about caring for others' needs
Most needs to learn that	Soliciting for other ideas may serve practical purposes; doing is as valuable as pondering

INTJ

Introverted Intuition With Extraverted Thinking

Experiences valuing when	Logical arguments provide a sufficient analysis to explain pros/cons and future courses of action
Expresses valuing by	Analyzing situations and providing a logical description of what has and is likely to happen
Most needs to learn that	A logical analysis may not be useful in various situations; accommodating behavior may be more effective in changing people's minds

TABLE 17 (CONTINUED)

TYPE PATTERNS IN APPLYING THE "GOLDEN RULE"

ISTP

Introverted Thinking With Extraverted Sensing

Experiences valuing when	Simple, practical actions are based on accurate information and a logical discussion
Expresses valuing by	Focusing on current experiences and providing a model to explain in concrete terms what has occurred
Most needs to learn that	People bring in personal histories and expectations that have nothing to do with the moment and that affect decisions made and actions taken

INTP

Introverted Thinking With Extraverted Intuition

Experiences valuing when	Models and frameworks are discussed as being possible
Expresses valuing by	Giving you attention to make your case and explain your situation
Most needs to learn that	Self-disclosure is an important aspect of relationships

ISFP

Introverted Feeling With Extraverted Sensing

Experiences valuing when	Personal, hands-on assistance is provided
Expresses valuing by	Gently encouraging others to act on some topic and then quietly going about doing what they believe needs to be done
Most needs to learn that	Neither gentleness nor beliefs alter the way some people act and reason out situations; being tough and questioning can be very helpful

INFP

Introverted Feeling With Extraverted Intuition

Experiences valuing when	Efforts are recognized as being offerings of personal meaning
Expresses valuing by	Writing notes, making calls, sending symbolic gifts
Most needs to learn that	Specific, logical, and critical analysis is very valuable and important to solving problems

TABLE 17 (CONTINUED)

TYPE PATTERNS IN APPLYING THE "GOLDEN RULE"

ESTP

Extraverted Sensing With Introverted Thinking

Experiences valuing when	Experiences affirm their competencies and abilities
Expresses valuing by	Involving others in activities and supporting appropriate challenges
Most needs to learn that	Quiet reflection is often a challenge and provides insights that cannot be gleaned from doing

ESFP

Extraverted Sensing With Introverted Feeling

Experiences valuing when	Actively involved in people-related events; offering to assist and being given the opportunity to do so
Expresses valuing by	Inviting others to share in some activity, meal, or conversation about current personal situations
Most needs to learn that	Not being included does not indicate dislike or disregard; some people function best alone

ENFP

Extraverted Intuition With Introverted Feeling

Experiences valuing when	Opportunities to share ideas and to openly reveal values and commitments are provided
Expresses valuing by	Offering various ideas and strategies for addressing a situation; sending mementos of experiences and conversations
Most needs to learn that	Tough, critical business rules for making decisions are ways of improving others' situations

ENTP

Extraverted Intuition With Introverted Thinking

Experiences valuing when	Questioning is encouraged and ideas are debated
Expresses valuing by	Showing a keen verbal interest in conversations
Most needs to learn that	Patient unfolding of information may provide more useful information than answers to questions

TABLE 17 (CONTINUED)

TYPE PATTERNS IN APPLYING THE "GOLDEN RULE"

ESTJ

Extraverted Thinking With Introverted Sensing

Experiences valuing when   Logical reasons for certain actions are acknowledged and supported

Expresses valuing by   Providing a detailed account of an experience

Most needs to learn that   Vision and relationships that are articulated and reinforced may be more useful at times than facts, details, and logic

---

ENTJ

Extraverted Thinking With Introverted Intuition

Experiences valuing when   Ideas are critiqued and suggestions are provided

Expresses valuing by   Offering new perspectives and more global views

Most needs to learn that   Emotional warmth and interpersonal concern are the grease of relationships that eventually enable ideas to become realities

---

ESFJ

Extraverted Feeling With Introverted Sensing

Experiences valuing when   Demonstrative caretaking behavior is evident

Expresses valuing by   Sympathizing with others and acting on beliefs about a situation

Most needs to learn that   Clarifying a theory or model and focusing on global issues may provide an important basis of relationships

---

ENFJ

Extraverted Feeling With Introverted Intuition

Experiences valuing when   Ideas that are shared are recognized and noted in conversation

Expresses valuing by   Seeking opportunities to discuss situations and to check out perceptions of events

Most needs to learn that   The importance of getting the facts straight and of making sure ideals are presented in a logical fashion

---

8

BEYOND PATTERNS AND TYPES

Being True to Ourselves

hen naturalist Merlin Tuttle learned of a plan to exterminate a million freetail bats that had taken up residence under an Austin, Texas, overpass, he launched a no-holds-barred campaign to educate nearby residents about the importance and value of bats. Tuttle proved to officials and many citizens that bats were not only benign but essential to the local economy because they consume millions of insects that otherwise would either destroy local farm products or necessitate the use of costly and harmful insecticides. He further demonstrated that insect infestations could reduce tourism.[47]

As a result, evening picnickers in Austin today take up posts close to the overpass to watch the bats' nightly emergence from under the bridge, cheering them on as nature's heroes. Tuttle was driven by the belief that if people understood the true nature of the bat and its importance to them, they would change their behavior, and he was right; through education and awareness, the situation was turned on its head and the once-feared bats are now celebrated.

If people's attitudes and behavior toward bats can change, perhaps the way they interact with others of their own species can change, too. Understanding psychological type can help. Tolerance and acceptance are worthwhile goals, and making even one small adjustment in your interactions—simply asking other people what they really mean before reacting to them—will have made this book worth reading for you and worth writing for us. As should be obvious by now, we think of type as an instructor for goodwill and for a general improvement in human relations.

Our Journey

Before writing this book, we asked ourselves: "What do we know for certain about behavior and psychological type?" There are many stories, anecdotes, and casual observations about type, but we wanted empirical data, not speculation. While anecdotes serve a purpose, we wanted to explore observed behaviors that are expressions of type, rather than stories about type. Besides remaining true to the data, we wanted to remain true to Carl Jung's theory of psychological type. As we traveled down this path, two things became increasingly clear.

First was the alarming realization that both psychological type as conceived by Carl Jung and Isabel Myers, and many of the individuals who are exposed to it, are being grossly abused by some popular applications of the theory through the improper use of the *Myers-Briggs Type Indicator* personality inventory. Too many individuals come away from their exposure to the MBTI thinking that their results are better or worse than others, or that type necessarily causes behavior. Such notions are directly contrary to the most fundamental tenets of type theory, which state firmly that no type is inherently more worthy than another and that preferences do not cause behavior. It's an abuse of type theory to use it to excuse unacceptable behavior ("You can't expect me to be prompt, that's not my type"), to explain poor performance ("I guess we made a mistake putting that type in the repossession department"), to blame others ("If you'd kept your head out of the clouds and paid attention to the details we wouldn't be in this mess"), to project onto others' motivations ("Folks of your type are only concerned with the bottom line!"), and to predict individual competencies ("I only hire secretaries of a certain type").

Our second realization was that while there are many empirical data points to support type theory and to explore behaviors, the complexity and richness of human experience make the exploration messy. Many of those who have fallen into the murky waters mentioned above do so out of a desire for type and the MBTI inventory to produce a neat and orderly framework of mutually exclusive types with which they can explain and predict human behavior. The reality is, of course, that neither the theory nor the MBTI inventory were designed for such a thing. Jung himself said, "The purpose of a psychological typology is not to classify human beings into types. This in itself would be pretty pointless."[48] So, after we waded into the messiness and complexity, our journey of research and reflection led us to the many levels and applications of type explicated in this book. We hope you have found each level rich with new insights about yourself and others that move you one step closer not only to understanding differences among people, but toward valuing those differences.

Life Is the Text; Type Is the Subtext

Life is the text: How we live it, revel in it, destroy it, and play out our individual stories is where the true value of type resides. As one subtext among many, psychological type gives us directions through life which we can, if we choose, ignore or keep in the background. Indeed, it is difficult to take such personal topics seriously when wars abound, people are starving, economies are in shambles, and governments around the world are on the brink. Yet if we can improve our ability to work with others, we can contribute to the improvement of everyone.

If we can teach children, young adults, and colleagues by example to communicate more effectively, develop more completely, and truly value others, then we are contributing to the welfare of us all. The lessons of type can help us achieve these goals if we will learn them and use them.

After leading thousands of individuals through seminars on psychological type, we are confident that many people learned in them for the first time that the way their minds work is normal, healthy, and (as we say in the South) just fine. Many have said, "If only I had known about this before, I would have done things differently"—meaning they would have managed difficult situations more effectively and more humanely than they did. Unfortunately, we are equally convinced that for most people the insight stops after the introduction. They learn about preferences and learn various type dynamics, and then fail to use them to their potential. Rare is the situation where individuals really work through the meaning of these basic concepts, and rarer still is the application of the concepts so that they actually change behavior.

Throughout this book we have argued that type is a very powerful model which explains the structure of our mental processes: we perceive and we judge, we extravert and we introvert, and we live in particular ways that create patterns. Like a watermark in fine stationery, type is embedded in the fabric of our personality. Our challenge is to remember to look for differences as part of our efforts to communicate with, motivate, and express our value for others. We must also find dignity in our own type as we work to develop our strengths and navigate the obstacles and opportunities of adulthood. Once you have been given the gift of understanding that type offers, it then becomes your responsibility to recognize the importance and contributions of all people who see the world differently from you—those whose stationery bears a different but equally exquisite watermark.

Type is in the background, never the foreground, of human relations. Ultimately, the text written over the watermark tells the story. The story is made up of experiences, traits and tendencies, situational factors, and a host of forces, most of which we cannot readily access through conversation. But when we know to look beyond the text to the watermark, we may begin to understand the preferred expressions, the limitations of perception, and the needs such limitations engender.

At a minimum, psychological type provides models for two very important insights into human nature. First is a model for understanding human differences that provides hypotheses about people different from ourselves but that doesn't value one type over another. Second is a model that provides basic questions to help us solve problems in any situation or interaction.

As a constructive model of human differences, type demonstrates that whenever we are involved in an interaction, there are several forces at work that both aid and hinder communication. For example, type informs us that some people need to talk out the issues and steps they see in order to gain clarity, while others simply tell what they have concluded. Type suggests that, when making decisions, some of us rely on facts and others on possibilities; an analytical decision is as important as a choice made in tune with a network of associations, so the only thing that matters is what response is appropriate in a given situation. In short, type allows us to understand differences, which invites us to consider another set of questions before jumping to conclusions.

Consider the outgoing parent who comes to understand that his or her careful, cautious, contained child is not afraid of challenges but goes about them differently. When the parent not only understands the difference, but acts in ways to affirm rather than change the child's style, the most important lesson of type has been learned. The teacher who knows that some kids need to connect with an overall plan before they complete a problem or task, and whose teaching style reflects that knowledge, has learned the power of type in motivating others. The boss who begins to recognize that employees are motivated by different things and interactions, and who behaves differently as a result, has started to understand the practical usefulness of type. Things that differ are not necessarily better or worse than one another; the dogwood and the cherry are different trees, but both flower and are beautiful in the spring.

Even if we reject type as an explanation of human differences and a template of mental functions, we can still take from it a few helpful questions applicable to home or work:

- To get work done and achieve a successful conclusion, do the people involved need an environment that provides regular stimulation and an openness to brainstorming and dialogue? To solve a problem, is regular access to information and feedback needed to increase the chances of making a good decision?

- Do you or those around you find clarity in situations by detaching yourself from surroundings and working through the information in your head before you share it? In problem solving, have you allowed enough time between exposure to information and required response for you and others to give your best effort?

- Are all the facts, as best they can be known and described, on the table? In problem solving, do you gather the hard and concrete data to give you the facts and current trends required to inform your decision?

- Have you considered being persuaded by future outcomes and potential results rather than current trends? In problem solving, do you examine the patterns in the data and strive to consider the largest, most global view?

- Have you delineated the pros and cons, weighed the alternatives by standard criteria, and measured the relative value of all the variables?

- Does your decision making take into account the effect of the ultimate decision on people, the probable long-term effects on their relationships, and the way it reflects on the values and connections you hold most dear?

- Have you set the deadline, the goal, the direction for your current activity?

- Have you provided opportunities to reopen a question, to reexamine a decision, and to pursue additional related information?

Ask each of these questions when you are working on a problem and you will find that you leave no stone unturned. Good, clean questions cut through the fog and can give each of us a way to address the most complex problems.

Our earnest hope is that as people retain their uniqueness and their special expressions of personality, they will recognize and honor the common bridges among all normal individuals regardless of nationality, race, gender, or any of the myriad other boundaries we place between us. We believe that psychological type is the bridge and provides an opportunity to move us individually and collectively forward in human relations. For many people, those bridges have been closed off far too long, creating invisible barriers to understanding and development. In the fast-changing, rapidly shrinking world now often known as the global village, type is a gift. It is the language that can open the doors between and among us so long as we honor its richness and complexity, which are a reflection of the wonder and uniqueness of us all.

Jung once said, based on his experience, that "people are incapable of understanding and accepting any point of view other than their own . . . forbearance, tolerance, and goodwill may help build a bridge over the chasm which lack of understanding opens between man and man."[49] We hope that we have given you ample evidence and motivation to find goodwill and tolerance within you, not just so you may understand others but so that you value them, honor them, and thank them for enriching your life. For in the end, a person's type is less important than how we treat each other, how we listen, and how we offer encouragement and show appreciation. Type merely gives us the impetus to recognize that there are differences worth paying attention to; this is the true gift and responsibility it leaves behind. Enjoy.

KNOWLEDGE PURCHASED

The Price of Understanding

Knowledge purchased without a loss of power
WORDSWORTH, *Prelude*

ife is a series of exchanges. It begins when sperm and ovum exchange their solitary existences for a union; the genes join, creating an exchange of energy, ions, and electrons. We exchange the air in our lungs for new air. We exchange our time for money and privilege. We exchange our life activity for one sort of perceived benefit or another. Our last exchange, our last breath, our last known expenditure occurs when we die. Between the first exchange and the last, there is a constant flow, a continual give and take that makes up life. Exchange means a relationship between two or more agents that share a currency—air, water, time, money. Perhaps our most precious expression of ourselves is the way we live our lives, but in all we do, we exchange something of ourselves to gain something else. The exchange, the relationship, is purposeful.

In modern times we gain knowledge through an exchange of time, activity, and sometimes cash. Most often our purpose in learning is to enhance our abilities to perform and produce, or simply to increase our satisfaction level. When we choose to learn about ourselves, we are confronted with information about how our behavior and ideas affect those around us. Sometimes we may not like what we discover; other times we are elated. But we always choose to participate in the exchange. We purchase knowledge about ourselves for the price of our energy, our time, and our awareness.

From the perspective of psychological type, when individuals learn, for example, that a preference for Introversion may incline

167

them to wait before responding to a stimulus, they have gained this information at the cost of time and money for the materials and interpreter's fee. In addition, if they believe the information is accurate, they are confronted with the knowledge that their behavior may affect others in unintended ways. Other such lessons would be gained from learning about any other personality preference or quality. For example, anyone who has been taught that people who pause before responding to a question are untrustworthy may experience Introverted behavior as untrustworthy. If persons with an Introverted preference decide this outcome is undesirable, they may seek to change; or they may say, "Tough! I can't change, so why worry about it?" They might even become very upset and distressed by the news. If they begin to use it as an excuse for behavior ("You can't expect an Introvert to do that!"), to blame others ("Just like a darned Extravert to misinterpret my behavior"), or to analyze others' behaviors, then a great deal has been exchanged for this newfound knowledge; namely, the Introvert will have given up approaching people openly, directly, freely, and without judgment, in exchange for a label. Even worse, the Introvert may have chosen to use a model or a system to forfeit responsibility for behavior. In such a case, the price of self-knowledge is too high; it leads to destructive ends and an ultimate loss of personal power.

But the currency you use can also be exchanged for a constructive way to think about human expressions and behaviors. If, for example, our Introverted role model from above learns that Introversion is a typical process of looking in before looking out, it may lead to awareness that this behavior puts some people off. If the Introvert decides not to change, it is with the full awareness that the behavior has consequences. But perhaps the Introvert decides to inform others of his typical process. He may come to realize that a simple comment like, "That's an interesting idea. Could I have some time to think about it before I give you my opinion?" can aid others in understanding his inward-looking behavior. This knowledge of one's own type can be used to gain the space and grace needed to interact successfully. In this example, it could be said that the knowledge purchased surpassed the price because the personal power gained through it is virtually immeasurable.

Psychological type is easy to learn and appears simple. Its simplicity leads some to quickly type other people, other behaviors, and other groups. This has led, regrettably, to the great overuse of type to label, pigeonhole, or limit people, creating rather than eliminating barriers to understanding. Thousands have exchanged their personal power and responsibility for growth, awareness, and understanding for a rigid model of personality. This is in direct opposition to what Jung and Myers intended. Perhaps more tragic yet are the individuals who reject type completely because it suggests that self-awareness is an important end, or because they deny having habits and patterns of mind. Those who exchange understanding in favor of pigeonholing, excuses, or blaming are like butterflies in a collector's net; their intellectual growth has ceased. Those who reject the whole concept save their money under a mattress; they're happy being caterpillars and don't want to think about growing into butterflies. They are equally ill-served by exposure to type. Both are stuck, limited, and closed.

Wordsworth was concerned in the *Prelude* with the experience of learning and living without sacrificing personal strength, personal wisdom, and individuality.[50] To learn, to gain knowledge without losing personal power, is to discover that one has an ability to perform certain kinds of magic without becoming enslaved by it. If individuals believe they have the knowledge that life is filled with trickery and greed, and in response give up hope for satisfying relationships, they have gained knowledge at the price of personal power. Some individuals who go to a psychologist to get tested are often looking for an excuse: They want to be labeled so that they no longer have responsibility for their behavior. For example, after diagnosis they may say, "I'm borderline XYZ, so what do you expect? I have no control over it!" If in response to that new knowledge the person gives up trying to address the problem, it might be said that the individual sacrificed power—the belief and effort to improve life—as a result of a distorted picture of himself.

Knowledge about oneself can be life-giving, as Socrates pointed out and Plato recounted in *The Republic*. As Socrates so well demonstrated in the allegory of the cave, realizing that you may have been looking at shadows rather than the real thing can be a remarkable discovery.[51] Such an insight forces you to recognize that there may still be more to learn and that you need to be mindful of the very human tendency to settle for the status quo. Awareness of this hazard increases your personal power. Discovering that you have a particular talent, for instance, may spur you to pursue other things, other ideas, other behaviors—in essence, to defy the status quo.

When people learn about type, our hope is that they exchange some ideas about themselves for a new perspective. Our goal is that they gain knowledge about themselves and others which, if used correctly—with tolerance and goodwill—will lead to new insights, choices, and opportunities for growth.

Using psychological type is difficult; it can invite categorization, stereotyping, and judgmental reactions. The most common problems can be summarized in three broad areas: when the right of self-determination of the individual is abused or ignored; when the knowledge level of the user or presenter of type is inadequate to the task; and when type is used in a context for which it was never intended (usually the result of an incompetent user of type).[52] These problems, however, are also opportunities for insight about appropriate applications of the type model and type instruments.

The Right of Self-Determination

Interpretation Settings

When presenting type or being introduced to psychological type, it is imperative that the value of the right of self-determination is honored at each juncture of interpretation. By right of self-determination we mean that when you receive the results of the MBTI or any other psychological instrument, you are the expert that interprets it. Your years of feedback from others and reflection on your own behavior take precedence over any other interpretation. It is important while exploring your type preferences to consider the role that situations play in the choices you make. Reflect on how learned behaviors, such as those from childhood (for example, always finish your work before you play), affect your judgments. Explore how developmental stretches influence your self-evaluation. If you are in the middle of a major life transition (new spouse, new job, new baby, or the like), how does this affect your thinking? In short, type should be presented in context to all the other major influences on behavior.

If you are a trainer or test interpreter, designing exercises that invite individuals to explore the various spheres of influence on behavior (such as life circumstances or work expectations) will help clients become clearer about which behaviors tend to be type-related and which are the byproducts of other forces. The same is true when using type for personal reflection. The point is to create an opportunity to evaluate information about behavior in all of its complexity and richness. If you were thinking about a career change, or if you help others to make career changes, you would not jump from one career to another simply because a psychological instrument suggested it; you would seek much more information—competencies required, general educational issues, work variety and pace, and the like. Likewise, when taking in information about your psychological type from an interpretation session, be sure to explore various influences on your behavior. Finally, you—the receiver of type instrument data—should determine your type preferences. Isabel Briggs Myers, creator of the MBTI instrument, would proclaim without hesitation that the Indicator results are a working hypothesis only.[53] You are the final judge. Anyone who says differently should be treated warily.

In the absence of a thorough examination of these multiple sources of behavior, type can be used to typecast others and to support various biases. For example, if you do not consider both when you express Extraversion and when you express Introversion, you may fall into the trap of either overvaluing your preference or limiting yourself. From that point on, it is easy to begin to ignore the contributions of other factors on your behavior.

Instrument Administration and Sharing of Results

Another aspect of self-determination is the taking of instruments in voluntary settings and the sharing of personal information as one decides appropriate. The benefits of any psychological instrument will be greatly enhanced if it is taken in a voluntary setting. The results are more likely to be accurate when people are confident that the results will not be shared without their permission, and when they feel free to answer questions honestly without regard for how they think they should or ought to respond. Everyone has a right to have personal information kept confidential and their results shared only with permission. For example, if you take a type instrument like the MBTI and the presenter posts your name and type without permission, your basic right of self-determination has been violated on two counts. First, you have not said such material could be shared. Second, until you determine whether the instrument accurately determined your type preferences, any pronouncements of your type are premature and unfounded.

Knowledge of the User/Interpreter

In personality assessment, no one should fall prey to the claim that an instrument designed to understand descriptive qualities or typical patterns can predict competence, excellence, or able expression of those qualities. Regrettably, many people who are qualified to purchase type instruments nevertheless are untrained in psychological type theory, models, or history; they are likely to treat the results of the MBTI or other type instruments as if they were measures of personality traits (meaning they could predict behavior), or as if they were akin to horoscopes. We have even heard about a professor who presents type concepts by drawing a bell curve of normalcy on the blackboard, as if something in the theory talks about abnormal behavior! Those who do not understand that healthy type development is about adaptation, flexibility, and fluidity in human responsiveness are likely to make an error by saying things like: "Introverted Thinkers always look for theoretical models." (Of course, within the context of psychological type only a very poorly developed type would always respond in any such way.) The heart of typology is a pattern within the multitude of potential behaviors. Trying to predict or determine what the behavior of an individual will be at any given instant is best left to the gods.

If material you read or listen to about type turns into predictions, ignore it! There simply are no empirical data to support the claim that all people of any type will always or nearly always respond to certain stimuli in certain ways. It is more rewarding to consider that types respond to situations with the mental functions required to manage them, and such adaptation may in fact result in behaviors quite atypical of the type.

Proper Context

Psychological type and type tools like the MBTI provide a very positive and constructive model to understand differences in the way individuals process and express information. Because of the assumptions of the model that all type mental functions are present and have potential within each person, it is inaccurate to make any job placement, team assignment, career advancement decision, or psychotherapeutic action based solely on type. While it is valuable to know one's type and what some typical reactions and blind spots may be in a particular situation, it is for developmental rather than diagnostic or managerial use. There is a very thin line between becoming aware of a rich model for growth and development and using that model to justify prejudices.

Individuals who do not understand the dynamic nature of type tend to see it in superficial ways. To consider type as some kind of educator's horoscope or parlor game is to have a poor understanding of the Extraverted–Introverted, Perception–Judgment balancing act the psyche carries out during every moment of conscious life. If all you do is look at the surface of a lake, you will miss the remarkable life underneath. Explorers of type need to be on guard against both pro-type and anti-type zealots; neither are likely to have more than a superficial understanding of typology.

A Time and a Place for Stories

If violating self-determination is the first sign that the price of learning about type is too high, and the second sign is overimportance assigned to it by incompetent users of type, beware of yet another sign. Hold suspect those who place overimportance on type and type instruments, and who then present materials that rely on speculative or anecdotal material for describing type. We all have stories that we feel are illustrative of type concepts. The issue here is identifying stories as stories and not presenting them as examples of a particular type. It is easy to get stories confused with reliable, research-based descriptors, and it is incumbent upon presenters to make it clear to the audience which is which.

Individuals who seek to read or conduct research and continue their education are more likely to provide a full picture of type and the implications of type in individual lives. Listeners and readers of psychological type material (or any psychological writings) should feel comfortable asking presenters about their education and experience with using type, perhaps asking if their training included more than one workshop. Presenters who have actively kept up with developments should feel free to provide lists of their involvement and their research related to type. It is time for the consumer to demand a higher standard for interpreters and presenters than simply having completed a qualifying program or a course in graduate school that enabled them to purchase psychological instruments. Without malice, individuals qualified to purchase type instruments by virtue of their education, but who have no relevant type training, are likely to go out into the work force with their new tools and models and proceed to expose them to individuals in inappropriate ways. The unfortunate outcome of all this unintentional incompetence is that a terrible price is extracted from some who are exposed to type: They develop a serious case of hardening of the categories. Like the arterial version that leads to death of the heart, this hardening leads to a death of the spirit.

Throughout this book we have argued that type is a splendid model for understanding human expressions and typical patterns of responses in communication. We have illustrated how multilayered the type model is and how remarkable it can be as a framework for supporting individual growth and development. Our work suggests that the empirical support exists for type to be seen as a serious model of human dispositions. While we are excited about the development of important type research and the growth in the use of type, our enthusiasm is tempered by the reality that for many people the price for self-discovery through learning about type has been much too high. This kind of unequal exchange of personal power for type knowledge is one that we would rather you not make.

NOTES

1. Myers, Isabel B., and McCaully, M. *Manual: A Guide to the Development and Use of the Myers-Briggs Type Indicator.* Palo Alto, Calif.: Consulting Psychologists Press, 1985.
2. Ibid., pp. 1–3.
3. Jung, Carl G. *Psychological Types.* Princeton, N. J.: Princeton University Press, 1971, pp. 330–405.
4. Myers, Isabel B., and Myers, P. *Gifts Differing.* Palo Alto, Calif.: Consulting Psychologists Press, 1980, pp. 69–76.
5. Jung, *Psychological Types*, pp. 333–336.
6. Myers and Myers, *Gifts Differing*, pp. 17–26.
7. Storm, H. *Seven Arrows.* Toronto: Ballantine Books, Random House.
8. Wilson, M., and Languis, M. "Differences in Brain Electrical Activity Patterns Between Introverted and Extraverted Adults," *Journal of Psychological Type, 18* (1989), pp. 14–23.
9. This issue is very important. Today most American psychologists consider Introversion a form of odd behavior. As an example, see Barrick, M. R., and Mount, M. K. "The Big Five Personality Dimensions and Job Performance," *Personnel Psychology,* 1991, pp. 1–23.
10. Jung, *Psychological Types*, pp. 359–361 and 368–370.
11. Coon, D. *Introduction to Psychology.* New York: West, 1989, pp. 256–275.
12. Jung, Carl G. *Modern Man in Search of a Soul.* New York: Harcourt Brace & World, 1933, pp. 74–94.
13. We have worked with 452 teams. These comments are the top four statements among all teams.
14. Myers and Myers, *Gifts Differing*, pp. 37–38.
15. Myers and McCaully, *Manual: A Guide to the Development and Use of the Myers-Briggs Type Indicator,* pp. 13–14.
16. Provost, J. *Procrastination.* Gainesville, Fla.: Center for the Application of Psychological Type, 1988.
17. Myers and McCaully, *Manual: A Guide to the Development and Use of the Myers-Briggs Type Indicator,* pp. 30–51.
18. Gough, Harrison, and Thorne, Avril, *Portraits of Type,* 1991; and Mitchell, Wayne, "A Test of Type Theory Using the TDI," *Journal of Psychological Type, 22,* (1991), pp. 15–26.
19. Ackerman, D. *A Natural History of the Senses.* New York: Random House, 1990, pp. 287–299.
20. Myers and Myers, *Gifts Differing*, pp. 83–116.

21. Jung, *Psychological Types,* pp. 405–407; Myers, Isabel B., *Introduction to Type,* Palo Alto, Calif.: Consulting Psychologists Press, 1993, pp. 8–23.

22. Myers and Myers, *Gifts Differing,* pp. 14–15.

23. Capra, F. *Tao of Physics.* Berkeley, Calif.: Shambala Press, 1975.

24. Jung, *Psychological Types,* pp. 175, 418–420.

25. Ibid., p. 516.

26. Intersecting research from psychological research publications such as *The Journal of Psychological Type,* articles in the database of the Center for Applications of Psychological Types.

27. Most of the time the general descriptions seem acceptable. However, there are sometimes considerable objections to the entire description.

28. Jung, *Modern Man in Search of a Soul,* pp. 92–94.

29. Von Franz, M. L. "The Inferior Function," *Jung's Typology,* Spring Publication, 1971, pp. 3–67; Myers and McCaully, *Manual: A Guide to the Development and Use of the Myers-Briggs Type Indicator,* p. 18; Sharp, D. *Personality Types,* Toronto: Inner City Books, 1987, pp. 21–24; Jung, *Psychological Types,* p. 450.

30. For a full discussion of this aspect of the inferior function, see Quenk, N. *Beside Ourselves.* Palo Alto, Calif.: Consulting Psychologists Press, 1993.

31. Jung, *Psychological Types,* p. 450.

32. *The Wizard of Oz.* Victor Fleming, Director. Hollywood: Metro-Goldwyn-Mayer Pictures, 1939. Based on L. Frank Baum's *The Wonderful World of Oz* (1900).

33. Extensive work on this aspect of child development has been completed by Jerome Kagan, Ph.D., Harvard University Professor of Education. Review any child development research journal to follow his work.

34. Corlett, E., and Millner, N. *Navigating Midlife.* Palo Alto, Calif.: Consulting Psychologists Press, 1993.

35. McCall, M., et al. *The Lessons of Experience.* New York: Macmillan, 1988.

36. Eliot, T. S. "Little Gidding." *The Complete Poems and Plays.* New York: Harcourt Brace & World, 1971, pp. 138–145.

37. *Twelve Angry Men.* Sidney Lumet, Director. Hollywood: Metro-Goldwyn-Mayer, Henry Fonda and Reginald Rose, Producers (1957).

38. Jung, *Psychological Types,* pp. 290–294, 457–458.

39. Jung, Carl G. *On the Nature of the Psyche.* Princton, N.J.: Princeton University Press, 1960, pp. 134–135.

40. McAleer, G., and Knode, S. "Senior Military Leaders and the MBTI," 1995 Conference Proceedings: Conscious Choices, Unconscious Forces, Association for Psychological Type, APTX, Newport Beach, Calif., pp. 111–113.

41. Myers and McCaully, *Manual: A Guide to the Development and Use of the Myers-Briggs Type Indicator,* pp. 13–14.

42. Pearman, Roger R. "Diversity Denied: Type Bias in Manager Selection," paper presented at the eleventh biennial conference of the Association for Psychological Type, July 15, 1995, Kansas City, Mo.

43. Jung, Carl G. *Symbols of Transformation.* Princeton, N.J.: Princeton University Press, 1956, p. 440.

44. Spencer, P. U. *Who Speaks for Wolf.* Austin, Tex.: Tribe of Two Press, 1983.

45. Ibid., pp. 36–37.

46. Myers and Myers, *Gifts Differing,* p. 178.

47. Tuttle, M. D. "North American Bats." *National Geographic 188: 2* (1995), pp. 36–57.

48. Jung, *Psychological Types,* pp. 554–555.

49. Ibid., p. 489.

50. Wordsworth, W. Prelude, Book IX. In *Selected Poems.* Boston: Houghton Mifflin, 1965.

51. Hamilton, E. and Carins, eds. *Plato.* Princeton, N.J.: Princeton University Press, 1973.

52. Pearman, R. "Knowledge Purchased: Uses and Misuses of the MBTI." *Bulletin of Psychological Type.* Winter, 1993.

53. A statement frequently made as a summary of the type verification steps suggested in Myers and McCaully, *Manual: A Guide to the Development and Use of the Myers-Briggs Type Indicator,* pp. 52–61.

ABOUT THE AUTHORS

Roger R. Pearman and **Sarah C. Albritton** use psychological type and the MBTI in their work as trainers, consultants, and executive coaches. They work extensively with executive, manager, and associate teams to facilitate the use of synergy in problem solving and of interpersonal strengths to enhance team work. Roger is a corporate vice president for Key Risk Management Services, a subsidiary of the W. R. Berkley Corporation, and Sarah is a senior partner in Leadership Innovations, Inc. Roger is a past president of the Association for Psychological Type and 1995 winner of the Myers Research Award. Sarah has held leadership positions in the American College Personnel Association. Both are members of the training faculty of the Association for Psychological Type. Together they have developed training programs for international audiences, one of which was *The Seven Levels of Type*.

INDEX